400-CALORIE INSTANT POT®

GOOD HOUSEKEEPING

400-CALORIE INSTANT POT®

65+ EASY & DELICIOUS RECIPES

★ GOOD FOOD GUARANTEED ★

HEARST
books

HEARSTBOOKS

An Imprint of Sterling Publishing Co., Inc.
1166 Avenue of the Americas
New York, NY 10036

ISBN 978-1-61837-312-0

The Good Housekeeping Cookbook Seal guarantees that the recipes in this publication meet the strict standards of the Good Housekeeping Institute. The Institute has been a source of reliable information and a consumer advocate since 1900 and established its seal of approval in 1909. Every recipe in this publication has been tested until perfect for ease, reliability, and great taste by the Good Housekeeping Test Kitchen.

Distributed in Canada by Sterling Publishing Co., Inc.
c/o Canadian Manda Group, 664 Annette Street
Toronto, Ontario M6S 2C8, Canada
Distributed in Australia by NewSouth Books
University of New South Wales, Sydney, NSW 2052, Australia

For information about custom editions, special sales, and premium and corporate purchases, please contact Sterling Special Sales at 800-805-5489 or specialsales@sterlingpublishing.com.

Manufactured in China

2 4 6 8 10 9 7 5 3 1

sterlingpublishing.com
goodhousekeeping.com

Cover design by Scott Russo
Interior design by Nancy Singer
Photography credits on page 126

Contents

Foreword

Love the Instant Pot? We do, too. If you're already using one, you know how it can give food rich flavor in a fraction of the time of other cooking methods.

The Instant Pot is truly a one-pot wonder. In addition to cooking delicious dinners in less time, it can cook rice, make yogurt, hard-cook eggs, steam veggies, keep food warm, and more. It's no wonder that Amazon sold more than 300,000 pots just on Prime Day in 2018! What started as one of the buzziest appliances of the decade is now a part of millions of kitchens and has an astonishing social media following.

In our first *Instant Pot® Cookbook,* we took a broad look at the appliance's powers for both slow and pressure-cooking. The more we cooked, the more we discovered. And with your input (we know you love the pressure function!), we've partnered with Instant Pot again to create a new collection of tested-'til-perfect recipes in the Good Housekeeping Test Kitchen. This new book takes you from breakfast through dinner and features more than sixty-five delicious recipes for meals under 400 calories, all using the pressure function.

While testing recipes, one of the things we discovered is that the Instant Pot does a fantastic job on eggs. Whether you want to make a custardy overnight French toast or simple hard-cooked eggs, the pot delivers. Ditto on rich flavorful chicken broth, a big batch of tomato sauce, risotto, polenta, spaghetti squash, and tender creamy beans (hello, hummus)—even if you forgot the overnight soak!

Browse the chapters and see that all your low-and-slow favorites are here, too: hearty Pasta Fagioli with Sausage, Coq au Vin, No-Time Tikka Masala, Arroz Con Pollo, plus stews, braises, chilis, and more. But now you can achieve the same delicious flavor in a fraction of the time.

And if you are new to the Instant Pot craze, we know that trying a new device can be a little daunting. Our introduction provides easy-to-use instructions that will ensure great results.

So take the pressure off you and turn up the pressure in the pot! These recipes will have you enjoying delicious, healthy meals in no time.

The editors of *Good Housekeeping*

CUBAN-STYLE PULLED PORK
WITH OLIVES
(PAGE 104)

The Instant Pot Guide
WHAT IS THE INSTANT POT?

The Instant Pot is a multicooker that combines the benefits of multiple kitchen appliances in one space-saving machine. It functions as a pressure cooker and slow cooker as well as a sauté pan, rice cooker, yogurt maker, and steamer. It also has a function that keeps your prepared meal warm, and newer models include other features as well. With the press of a button, the Instant Pot has simplified everyday cooking by reducing cooking times and ensuring nutritious meals are on the table even faster.

INSTANT POT PREPARATION

Before using the Instant Pot, make sure to follow these procedures.

1. Install the condensation collector at the rear of the cooker. Place the steam release handle on the lid.

2. To remove the lid, hold the handle, turn the lid counterclockwise, and lift.

3. Remove the inner pot from the cooker, unless you're using the sauté function. If using this function, the next steps can proceed with the inner pot in the cooker.

4. Add food and liquids to the inner pot as the recipe directs. If steaming, place the steamer rack on the bottom of the inner pot first.

5. Wipe the outside of the inner pot dry. Make sure there is no food debris on the cooking element.

6. Put the inner pot back into the cooker. Rotate slightly to ensure that it is seated correctly.

7. Make sure the sealing ring is properly seated in the sealing ring rack and there are no deformations. Do not attempt to repair a deformed ring rack.

8. To place the lid, reverse step 2. Place the lid on the cooker, align the ▲ mark on the lid with the unlock mark, and turn clockwise.

PRESSURE-COOKING IN THE INSTANT POT

Unlike your grandmother's stovetop pressure cooker, which had an unsafe reputation, the Instant Pot is designed to avoid common user errors and safety hazards of conventional pressure-cooking. Follow these procedures each time for proven results.

1. Connect the power cord. The LED display shows "OFF," indicating that it's in the standby state. Follow the Instant Pot Preparation steps (left).

2. Select a cooking program like Manual/Pressure Cook, Soup, Meat/Stew, Beans/Chili, and so on. The steam release handle should be in the Sealing position. Once a program key is pressed, its indicator lights up. Within 10 seconds after pressing a program key, you can still select other program keys and adjust cooking time.

3. Select the cooking pressure. All programs besides Rice default to high

pressure. The Rice program defaults to low pressure, which operates at half the regular working pressure and can be used to avoid overcooking tender food such as vegetables.

4. Select the cooking time. You may use the Adjust key (except for Manual/Pressure Cook and Rice programs) to adjust cooking time. Press the Adjust key repeatedly to change between normal, less, and more modes, which will light up on the display. If necessary, change the cooking time with [+] and [–]. Press and hold the [+] or [–] key for faster changes.

5. Cooking automatically starts 10 seconds after the last key press. Three audible beeps will sound to indicate the cooking process has begun. The LED display shows "ON," indicating that the preheating state is in progress. Once the cooker reaches working pressure, the LED display changes from "ON" to the programmed cooking time. The cooking time counts down to indicate the remaining time in minutes.

6. When the pressure-cooking cycle finishes, the cooker beeps and automatically goes into the keep warm cycle, which can be used for up to 10 hours. After 10 hours, the cooker goes into standby state. Press Keep Warm/Cancel to stop the cycle and return the pot to its standby state.

RELEASING PRESSURE

There are two methods of releasing pressure when using the Instant Pot.

Quick Release: Turn the steam release handle to the Venting position to let steam out until the float valve drops down. Never pull out the steam release handle while releasing steam, as escaping steam is extremely hot and can cause scalds. For food with large liquid volume or starch content, use natural release instead, as thick liquid may splatter out.

Natural Release: Allow the cooker to cool down naturally until the float valve drops down. This may take 10 to 40 minutes, or even more, depending on the amount of food in the cooker. Place a wet towel on the lid to speed up cooling.

SAUTÉING IN THE INSTANT POT

1. Connect the power cord. The LCD displays "OFF," indicating that the cooker is in the standby state.

2. Select the sauté program. To change the cooking temperature, press the Sauté program key repeatedly to select between normal, less, and more. (See Cooking Program Options on page 12).

3. The preheating cycle starts automatically in 10 seconds after the last key is pressed. Three audible beeps will sound to indicate the working temperature is reached. The LED display shows "HOT," indicating you can add food to the inner pot.

4. When you have finished sautéing the food, press Cancel. The LCD displays "OFF," indicating the cooker is in the standby state.

INSTANT POT SAFETY TIPS

When pressure-cooking with the Instant Pot, there are important safety tips to keep in mind.

- Do not open the Instant Pot until the cooker has cooled and all internal pressure has been released. If the float valve is still up or the lid is difficult to turn, it is an indication that the cooker is still pressurized. Do not force it open.

- Make sure the steam release valve is in the Sealing position for all the pressure-cooking programs.

- Always check the steam release valve, float valve, and anti-block shield for clogging before use.

- For all pressure-cooking programs, the total amount of precooked food and liquid in the inner pot should not pass the ⅔ line. When cooking food that expands during cooking, such as rice, beans or vegetables, the inner pot should not pass the ½ line.

- Be aware that certain foods, such as applesauce, cranberries, pearl barley, and split peas can foam, froth, sputter, and clog the steam release. We recommend following specific instructions for cooking these dishes under pressure or they can be made using the Slow Cook function.

Cooking Program Options

Depending on the model of your Instant Pot, there are a variety of preprogrammed buttons for easy use. These are the most common programs.

PROGRAM	MODE	COOKING OPTION	NOTES
Bean/Chili	Less	Less soft texture	Choose different modes based on the desired bean texture.
	Normal	Soft texture	
	More	Very soft texture	
Egg	Less	Soft-boiled eggs	Preset times are intended for extra-large eggs. Adjust cooking time to account for different-size eggs.
	Normal	Medium-boiled eggs	
	More	Hard-boiled eggs	
Meat/Stew	Less	Soft meat texture	Choose different modes based on the desired meat texture.
	Normal	Very soft meat texture	
	More	Fall-off-the-bone meat texture	
Multigrain	Less	Wild rice, brown rice, mung beans, etc.	Choose the Less or Normal mode based on the type of grain and desired texture.
	Normal	Wild rice, brown rice, mung beans, etc.	
	More	Tough grains or a mixture of grains and beans	In newer models, this program includes 45 minutes of warm-water soaking time prior to 60 minutes of pressure-cooking.
Rice	Less	Al dente white rice	This is an automated cooking program. The LCD display will show "AUTO" until cooking countdown time starts.
	Normal	Normal-texture white rice	
	More	Softer-texture white rice	

PROGRAM	MODE	COOKING OPTION	NOTES
Sauté	Less	Simmering, thickening, and reducing liquids	Safety is important. Never have the lid on while sautéing. After 30 minutes, the pot will enter the standby state.
	Normal	Pan-searing or sautéing	
	More	Stir-frying or browning	
Slow Cook	Less	Corresponds to a LOW setting in a temperature-controlled slow cooker	As a non-pressure-cooking program, you may also use the Instant Pot glass lid as an option.
	Normal	Corresponds to a MEDIUM setting in a temperature-controlled slow cooker	
	More	Corresponds to a HIGH setting in a temperature-controlled slow cooker	
Soup/Broth	Less	Soup without meat	The soup/broth will remain clear due to lack of boiling motion under pressure-cooking.
	Normal	Soup with meat	
	More	Rich bone broth	
Steam	Less	Vegetables	Use the trivet provided to elevate the food above water. Use the quick release method to prevent food from overcooking.
	Normal	Fish and seafood	
	More	Meat	

STEEL-CUT OATMEAL
(PAGE 16)

1 | Breakfast, Snacks & Sides

Is your Instant Pot your go-to cooking tool for breakfast prep? If not, you may want to reconsider. You can make custardy French toast, tender frittatas, and foolproof hard-cooked eggs. And if you're a fan of steel cut oats, this device allows you to make a big batch and eat it all week!

We also have delicious options for serving hard-cooked eggs. Try amping up deviled eggs with Ham & Cheese or the very craveable Miso-Ginger, Caesar, or Guacamole fillings. Need a side to go with your roasted or grilled main dish? Make one of our Mashed Potato options: they are all crowd pleasers. Plus, dried beans cook up beautifully in the Instant Pot, and if you have leftovers, you can turn them into soup!

Steel-Cut Oatmeal

With this recipe you will have super-creamy, fuss-free oatmeal every time! Make a double batch and reheat individual servings in the microwave on high for 1½–2 minutes. See photo on page 14.

PREP: 5 MINUTES   TOTAL: 25 MINUTES

1 cup whole milk

1 cup steel-cut oats

¼ teaspoon kosher salt

2 teaspoons coconut oil or butter

1½ cups water

1. In the Instant Pot, combine the milk, oats, salt, coconut oil, and water. Cover and lock the lid. Select Manual/Pressure Cook and cook at high pressure for 5 minutes. Once the cooking is complete, release the pressure using the natural release function for 15 minutes, then release the remaining pressure using a quick release. Stir the oats and serve. Makes 3¼ cups.

SERVES 4: About 225 calories, 9g protein, 32g carbohydrates, 7g fat (4g saturated), 5g fiber, 146mg sodium.

TIP

Receive an extra boost of nutrients with slivered almonds, blueberries, and bananas on top!

FUN FLAVORS

Spinach & Egg

Top one serving of cooked oatmeal with **½ cup chopped fresh spinach, 1 tablespoon chopped green onion, 1 fried egg, 1 tablespoon grated Parmesan,** and **ground black pepper.**

SERVES 1: About 345 calories, 17g protein, 34g carbohydrates, 16g fat (6g saturated), 6g fiber, 345mg sodium.

Maple Bacon

Top one serving of cooked oatmeal with **1 cooked and crumbled bacon strip, 2 tablespoons chopped apple,** and **2 teaspoons pure maple syrup.**

SERVES 1: About 315 calories, 12g protein, 43g carbohydrates, 11g fat (5g saturated), 5g fiber, 285mg sodium.

Mango & Coconut

Top one serving of cooked oatmeal with **⅓ cup diced mango, 1 tablespoon toasted coconut, 2 teaspoons orange marmalade,** and **a pinch of ground allspice or nutmeg.**

SERVES 1: About 325 calories, 10g protein, 51g carbohydrates, 10g fat (6g saturated), 6g fiber, 156mg sodium.

Overnight French Toast Casserole

If you don't have time to plan ahead, this easy breakfast can also be prepared at the last minute.

PREP: 10 MINUTES   TOTAL: 25 MINUTES, PLUS OVERNIGHT TO CHILL

6 slices firm white bread, quartered

3 large eggs

¼ teaspoon ground cinnamon

⅛ teaspoon ground nutmeg

Pinch of kosher salt

¼ cup packed brown sugar

1 cup whole milk

½ teaspoon vanilla extract

1½ cups water

1 tablespoon butter, melted

1 tablespoon pure maple syrup

1. Layer the bread pieces in a 7-inch (1½-quart) straight-sided heatproof baking dish or soufflé dish.

2. In a bowl, whisk together the eggs, cinnamon, nutmeg, salt, and 3 tablespoons of the brown sugar in a bowl until blended. Whisk in the milk and vanilla; pour it over the bread. Cover with foil and refrigerate overnight.

3. Make an aluminum foil sling and set it aside (see Tip). In the Instant Pot, insert the steamer rack and add the water. Using the foil sling, set the baking dish on the rack in the pot. Fold down the ends of the sling.

4. Cover and lock the lid. Select Manual/Pressure Cook and cook at high pressure for 12 minutes. Meanwhile, in a small bowl, stir together the melted butter, maple syrup, and the remaining 1 tablespoon brown sugar. Once cooking is complete, release the pressure by using the natural release function for 5 minutes, then release the remaining pressure by using a quick release. Lift out the dish using the sling and remove the foil cover. Spoon and spread the butter mixture on top.

SERVES 4: About 280 calories, 10g protein, 35g carbohydrates, 10g fat (5g saturated), 1g fiber, 308mg sodium.

TIP

To make an aluminum foil sling, fold a 24-inch piece of foil in half lengthwise and then in half again lengthwise. Center it under the dish or item you are placing in the cooker and fold the ends down a few times to make handles. Use the handles to transport the item into the cooker. Then fold the handles down, so that they are below the rim of the insert, and clear the cover.

Hard-Cooked Eggs

Pressure-cooking makes easy work of peeling hard-boiled eggs.

PREP: 5 MINUTES   TOTAL: 10 MINUTES, PLUS CHILLING

6 large eggs

1 cup water

Place the eggs on a rack or steamer basket in the Instant Pot. Add the water. Cover and lock the lid. Select Manual/Pressure Cook and cook at high pressure for 5 minutes. Once cooking is complete, release the pressure by using a quick release. Transfer to a bowl to cool and store refrigerated for up to 3 days.

SERVES 6: About 70 calories, 6g protein, 0g carbohydrates, 5g fat (2g saturated), 0g fiber, 70mg sodium.

Beet-Dyed Eggs

In a medium saucepan, combine **8 cups water**, **4 medium beets** (peeled and thinly sliced), **2 cups distilled white vinegar**, and **1 tablespoon salt** and bring to boiling on high. Reduce heat to simmering; cook 20 minutes. Cool liquid completely. Remove and reserve beets for another use. Transfer the pickling liquid to a gallon-size resealable bag set in a large bowl; add **12 peeled hard-boiled eggs**. Squeeze the air out of the bag and seal, making sure the eggs are submerged. Refrigerate for 1 hour. Remove the eggs from the liquid and blot completely dry with paper towels before using.

TIP

The Beet-Dyed Eggs can be used when making Horseradish Beet Devilish Eggs (right).

Devilish Eggs

These five variations are devilish and delish! To prep, peel and halve **12 large hard-boiled eggs** lengthwise. Transfer yolks to medium bowl and mash with a choice of flavoring below. Pipe mixture into whites and garnish as directed.

HORSERADISH BEET

3 tablespoons mayonnaise + 1 cup very well drained prepared horseradish + 1 tablespoon Worcestershire sauce + ½ teaspoon salt

Pipe into Beet-Dyed Egg whites (see facing page); garnish with fresh dill.

SERVES 24: About 55 calories, 3g protein, 2g carbohydrates, 4g fat (1g saturated), 0g fiber, 171mg sodium.

CAESAR

½ cup mayonnaise + ¼ cup grated Parmesan cheese + 2 tablespoons lemon juice + 2 teaspoons Dijon mustard + 1 small clove garlic, crushed with garlic press

Garnish filled eggs with broken Parmesan crisps, pepper, and fresh basil.

SERVES 24: About 75 calories, 4g protein, 1g carbohydrates, 6g fat (2g saturated), 0g fiber, 94mg sodium.

GUACAMOLE

1 small avocado + ¼ cup mayonnaise + ¼ cup finely chopped fresh cilantro + 1 very small shallot, finely chopped + 2 tablespoons lime juice + ½ teaspoon salt

Garnish filled eggs with broken tortilla chips and thinly sliced serrano chilies.

SERVES 24: About 65 calories, 3g protein, 1g carbohydrates, 5g fat (1g saturated), 0g fiber, 89mg sodium.

MISO-GINGER

½ cup mayonnaise + 2 tablespoons white or yellow miso + 1 teaspoon grated peeled fresh ginger + ½ teaspoon ground black pepper + ¼ teaspoon sugar

Garnish filled eggs with snipped chives and finely julienned fresh ginger.

SERVES 24: About 72 calories, 3g protein, 1g carbohydrates, 6g fat (1g saturated), 0g fiber, 100mg sodium.

HAM & CHEESE

½ cup mayonnaise + ½ cup finely grated sharp Cheddar cheese + 3 tablespoons drained sweet relish + 2 slices deli ham, finely chopped + 1 tablespoon spicy brown mustard + ¼ teaspoon salt

SERVES 24: About 83 calories, 4g protein, 1g carbohydrates, 7g fat (2g saturated), 0g fiber, 131mg sodium.

Kale, Tomato & Goat Cheese Frittata

Shop your fridge and get creative. Add chopped leftovers, a blend of cheeses, and/or fresh herbs to the egg-milk mixture.

PREP: 15 MINUTES   TOTAL: 35 MINUTES

1½ cups frozen chopped kale

1½ cups plus 3 tablespoons water

8 large eggs

½ cup whole milk

¾ teaspoon kosher salt

⅛ teaspoon ground black pepper

1 ripe medium tomato, seeded and chopped

2 tablespoons snipped fresh chives

2 ounces goat cheese, coarsely crumbled

1. In a microwave-safe bowl, combine the kale and 3 tablespoons of the water. Cover with vented plastic wrap and cook in the microwave oven on high for 5 minutes. Drain and let cool.

2. Spray a 1½-quart (7-inch) heatproof soufflé dish with cooking spray.

3. In a medium bowl, beat the eggs, milk, salt, and pepper with fork until well blended. Stir in the tomato, chives, and kale. Pour the mixture into the prepared baking dish. Sprinkle with crumbled goat cheese. Cover the dish with foil.

4. Make an aluminum foil sling and set it aside (see Tip, page 17). In the Instant Pot, insert the steamer rack and add 1½ cups water. Place the baking dish on the foil sling and set it on the rack in the pot. Fold down the ends of the sling. Cover and lock the lid. Select Manual/Pressure Cook and cook at high pressure for 30 minutes. Once cooking is complete, release the pressure by using a quick release.

5. Using pot holders, carefully lift the dish out using the sling. Uncover and check that the center of the frittata is set. If not, cover with foil and return it to pot. Cover and lock the lid. Select Manual/Pressure Cook and cook at high pressure 3 minutes. Release the pressure by using a quick release. Uncover the frittata and let stand 10 minutes before serving.

SERVES 4: About 220 calories, 17g protein, 5g carbohydrates, 14g fat (6g saturated), 2g fiber, 596mg sodium.

Pepper & Cheddar Frittata

Omit the kale, tomato, chives, and goat cheese. Chop **1 red bell pepper** and **1 medium onion**. In the Instant Pot, select the sauté function and adjust the heat to more. Cook the bell pepper and onion in **2 teaspoons olive oil** for 5 minutes, or until softened and lightly browned, stirring occasionally. Transfer the vegetables to a plate. Hit cancel to turn off the sauté function. Prepare the egg mixture as directed in steps 2 and 3. Stir in the pepper mixture and **½ cup shredded sharp Cheddar cheese**. Using the sling, set the dish on the steamer rack and cook as directed in steps 4 and 5, for 28 minutes, or until the egg is set in the center.

SERVES 4: About 260 calories, 17g protein, 7g carbohydrates, 18g fat (7g saturated), 2g fiber, 603mg sodium.

Candied Carrots

Cooking these root vegetables on a steamer rack helps retain more of their nutritional value.

PREP: 10 MINUTES   **TOTAL: 35 MINUTES**

1½ pounds carrots

1 lemon

1½ cups water

1½ tablespoons butter

 cup brown sugar

½ teaspoon kosher salt

1. Cut each carrot crosswise in half. Cut each thick portion lengthwise in half (or quarters if large). From the lemon, grate 1 teaspoon zest and squeeze 1 teaspoon juice and set aside.

2. In the Instant Pot, insert the steamer rack and add the water. Place the carrots on the rack. Cover and lock the lid. Select Manual/Pressure Cook function and cook at high pressure for 4 minutes. Once cooking is complete, release the pressure using a quick release. Remove the steamer rack with the carrots and discard the water in the pot.

3. Combine the butter, brown sugar, salt, and carrots in the pot. Select the sauté function and cook, stirring gently, until the sugar has dissolved and the carrots are glazed, about 5 minutes. Stir in the lemon zest and juice.

SERVES 6: About 100 calories, 1g protein, 19g carbohydrates, 3g fat (2g saturated), 3g fiber, 255mg sodium.

FUN FLAVORS

Ginger Candied Carrots

Prepare as directed, but add **1 teaspoon grated peeled fresh ginger** in step 3.

SERVES 6: About 100 calories, 1g protein, 19g carbohydrates, 3g fat (2g saturated), 3g fiber, 255mg sodium.

Candied Parsnips

Prepare as directed, but substitute **1½ pounds parsnips**, peeled, for the carrots. Cook at high pressure for 3 minutes in step 2.

SERVES 6: About 135 calories, 1g protein, 26g carbohydrates, 3g fat (2g saturated), 5g fiber, 195mg sodium.

Beets in Orange Vinaigrette

Beets seem to take forever when roasting in the oven.
In the Instant Pot, they are done in 20 minutes!

PREP: 15 MINUTES   TOTAL: 45 MINUTES

2 cups water

6 medium beets (2 pounds)

½ teaspoon grated orange zest

¼ cup fresh orange juice

1 small clove garlic, crushed with a garlic press

½ teaspoon kosher salt

¼ teaspoon ground black pepper

2 tablespoons olive oil

¼ cup fresh cilantro leaves

1. In the Instant Pot, insert the steamer rack and add the water. Set the beets on the rack. Cover and lock the lid. Select Manual/Pressure Cook and cook at high pressure for 20 minutes. Once cooking is complete, release the pressure by using the natural release function.

2. Remove the beets from the pot and let stand 5 minutes, or until they're cool enough to handle but still warm. Rub off the skins with your hands. Cut the beets into wedges and place them on a platter.

3. In a small bowl, combine the orange zest, orange juice, garlic, salt, and pepper. Whisk in the olive oil. Drizzle the vinaigrette over the beets and sprinkle with cilantro.

SERVES 6: About 90 calories, 2g protein, 11g carbohydrates, 5g fat (1g saturated), 3g fiber, 240mg sodium.

TIP

There's a trick to peeling beets easily: Run them under cool water while still warm and rub off the skin with your hands.

Basic Mashed Potatoes

Depending on the moisture level in the potatoes, the time of year they are harvested, and their age, you may not need to add all the milk. Add gradually and assess as you go.

PREP: 20 MINUTES   TOTAL: 40 MINUTES

3 pounds baking potatoes, peeled and cut into 1½-inch pieces

1 cup water

4 tablespoons butter, cut into pieces

1½ teaspoons kosher salt

¾ cup whole milk, warmed

1. In the Instant Pot, combine the potatoes and water. Cover and lock the lid. Select Manual/Pressure Cook and cook at high pressure for 8 minutes. Once cooking is complete, release the pressure by using a quick release function.

2. Select the keep warm function. Drain the potatoes and return them to the pot. Add the butter and salt and mash the potatoes. Gradually add the warm milk, mashing the potatoes until smooth and fluffy.

SERVES 8: About 185 calories, 3g protein, 29g carbohydrates, 7g fat (4g saturated), 2g fiber, 422mg sodium.

Parsnip & Potato Mash

Prepare as directed, but substitute **1 pound parsnips**, peeled and cut into 1-inch pieces, for 1 pound potatoes and use only **¾ cup milk**.

SERVES 8: About 180 calories, 3g protein, 29g carbohydrates, 7g fat (4g saturated), 4g fiber, 425mg sodium.

FUN FLAVORS

Cheesy Chive Mash

Fold **2 cups shredded extra-sharp Cheddar cheese** and **¼ cup snipped fresh chives** into Basic Mashed Potatoes until well mixed.

SERVES 8: About 295 calories, 10g protein, 29g carbohydrates, 16g fat (9g saturated), 2g fiber, 602mg sodium.

Zingy Bacon Mash

Fold **6 strips crumbled cooked bacon**, **3 tablespoons bottled white horseradish**, and **3 tablespoons chopped fresh flat-leaf parsley** into Basic Mashed Potatoes until well mixed.

SERVES 8: About 220 calories, 6g protein, 30g carbohydrates, 9g fat (5g saturated), 2g fiber, 549mg sodium.

Spicy 'n' Smoky Mash

Fold **2 cups frozen corn, thawed, ⅔ cup reduced-fat sour cream**, and **2 tablespoons chopped chipotles in adobo sauce** into Basic Mashed Potatoes until well mixed.

SERVES 8: About 250 calories, 6g protein, 37g carbohydrates, 10g fat (6g saturated), 3g fiber, 467mg sodium.

Bistro White Beans

Forget to soak your beans overnight? Here's a quick soak method for the Instant Pot: Combine 8 cups water and 1 pound beans in the pot and cook at high pressure for 2 minutes. After a 10-minute natural release, rinse and drain the beans, then cook as directed.

PREP: 15 MINUTES   TOTAL: 25 MINUTES, PLUS SOAKING

1 package (16 ounces) great northern beans

1½ tablespoons butter

1 large onion, chopped

2 cloves garlic, slivered

1 can (14½ ounces) petite diced tomatoes

2 bay leaves

2 teaspoons kosher salt

3 sprigs fresh thyme

2 cups water

¼ teaspoon ground black pepper

1 teaspoon chopped fresh thyme leaves

1. Place the beans in a large bowl. Add enough cold water to cover by 2 inches. Let stand 8 hours or overnight. Drain and rinse well.

2. In the Instant Pot, using the sauté function, heat the pot for 1 to 2 minutes. Add the butter and chopped onion and cook, uncovered, for 5 minutes, or until softening. Add the garlic and cook 1 minute. Add the drained beans, tomatoes, bay leaves, salt, thyme sprigs, and water.

3. Cover and lock the lid. Select Manual/Pressure Cook and cook at high pressure for 20 minutes. Once cooking is complete, release the pressure by using the natural release function for 10 minutes, then release the remaining pressure by using a quick release. (The beans should be tender but still retain their shape.) Remove the bay leaves and thyme sprigs. Stir in the pepper and chopped thyme. Serve hot, warm, or at room temperature. Makes 8 cups.

SERVES 8: About 230 calories, 13g protein, 40g carbohydrates, 3g fat (2g saturated), 13g fiber, 625mg sodium.

Mashed Root Vegetables

You can customize this blend of root vegetables to your liking. Layer the toughest vegetables in the pot first, such as rutabaga, and then end with the potatoes.

PREP: 15 MINUTES   TOTAL: 35 MINUTES

¾ cup lower-sodium chicken broth, homemade (page 37) or store-bought, or water

2 pounds root vegetables, such as carrots, white turnips, rutabaga, or parsnips, peeled and cut into ¾-inch pieces

1 pound all-purpose potatoes, peeled and cut into 1½-inch pieces

2 cloves garlic, sliced

3 tablespoons butter, cut into pieces

¾ teaspoon kosher salt

¼ teaspoon ground black pepper

Pinch of ground nutmeg

1. Pour the broth into the Instant Pot; add the root vegetables, potatoes, and garlic. Cover and lock the lid. Select Manual/Pressure Cook and cook at high pressure for 8 minutes. Once cooking is complete, release the pressure by using a quick release.

2. Drain the vegetables, reserving the cooking liquid. Return the vegetables to the pot; add the butter, salt, pepper, and nutmeg. Mash until smooth, adding some of the reserved cooking liquid, if needed. Makes 4 cups.

SERVES 8: About 125 calories, 2g protein, 20g carbohydrates, 5g fat (3g saturated), 4g fiber, 280mg sodium.

Praline Sweet Potatoes

The natural sweetness and creaminess of the potatoes is enhanced by a sweet, crunchy pecan praline. If you like some spice, add a pinch of cayenne to the pecans along with the cinnamon.

PREP: 20 MINUTES   TOTAL: 45 MINUTES

3 tablespoons butter

½ cup pecans, coarsely chopped

2 tablespoons packed brown sugar

Pinch of cinnamon

1 cup water

3 pounds sweet potatoes, peeled and cut into 1½-inch chunks

1 teaspoon kosher salt

½ cup whole milk

TIP

If you like your potatoes smoother and fluffier, you can beat them with an electric mixer, providing the beaters are long enough to fit into the Instant Pot.

---

1. In a small nonstick skillet, melt 1 tablespoon of the butter over low heat. Add the pecans, brown sugar, and cinnamon. Cook 5 minutes, or until the pecans are lightly toasted and the sugar melts, stirring frequently. Turn the contents out onto a plate to cool.

2. Place the steamer rack in the Instant Pot. Add the water and sweet potatoes. Cover and lock the lid. Select Manual/Pressure Cook and cook at high pressure for 10 minutes.

3. While potatoes cook, break the candied pecans into small pieces.

4. Once cooking is complete, release the pressure by using a quick release. Protecting your hands with oven mitts, remove the steamer rack with the potatoes. Pour off and discard the water in the pot. Return the potatoes to the pot and add the remaining 2 tablespoons butter and the salt. Mash until smooth. Gradually add milk while mashing, until fluffy. Turn the potatoes into a serving dish and sprinkle with the pecans. Makes 5 cups.

SERVES 8: About 205 calories, 3g protein, 29g carbohydrates, 9g fat (3g saturated), 3g fiber, 318mg sodium.

Sweet & Smoky Spaghetti Squash

Cooking this squash in the Instant Pot means
ready-to-eat veggie noodles in no time!

PREP: 15 MINUTES   TOTAL: 55 MINUTES

1 medium spaghetti squash (2 pounds)

1 cup water

3 slices bacon, chopped

1 medium onion, chopped

2 tablespoons pure maple syrup

1 tablespoon cider vinegar

¾ teaspoon kosher salt

¼ teaspoon ground black pepper

1. Pierce the squash 12 times, all over, with the tip of a paring knife.

2. Place the steamer rack in the Instant Pot and add the water. Place the squash on the rack. Cover and lock the lid. Select Manual/Pressure Cook and cook at high pressure for 20 minutes. Once cooking is complete, release the pressure by using a quick release.

3. Transfer the squash to cutting board and let cool 10 minutes.

4. While the squash cools, remove the steamer rack from the pot and pour off the cooking water. Select the sauté function and add the bacon. Cook the bacon until browned, about 5 minutes, stirring frequently. Using a slotted spoon, transfer the bacon to a paper-towel-lined plate. Add the onion to the pot and cook 4 minutes, until softened and golden, stirring frequently. Add to the bacon.

5. Cut the squash in half lengthwise and scrape out the seeds. Using a fork, scrape out the squash pulp in long strands onto a serving platter. Add the bacon, onion, maple syrup, cider vinegar, salt, and pepper; toss with two forks to mix. Makes 5 cups.

SERVES 4: About 175 calories, 4g protein, 21g carbohydrates, 9g fat (3g saturated), 3g fiber, 529mg sodium.

Classic Hummus

Want to make the creamiest hummus ever? Our recipe uses baking soda, which softens the chickpea skins and produces an ultrasmooth spread. Make this recipe once and you'll never go back to store-bought.

PREP: 15 MINUTES   TOTAL: 45 MINUTES, PLUS STANDING

1½ cups dried chickpeas (half a 1-pound package)

1 teaspoon baking soda

8 cups water

2 teaspoons vegetable oil

4 cloves garlic

6 tablespoons fresh lemon juice

¾ teaspoon ground cumin

1¼ teaspoons kosher salt

¾ cup tahini

1. In the Instant Pot, combine the chickpeas, baking soda, and 4 cups of the water. Let stand at room temperature overnight. Drain the chickpeas (do not rinse) and return them to the pot, along with the oil and the remaining 4 cups water.

2. Cover and lock the lid. Select Manual/Pressure Cook and cook at high pressure for 20 minutes. Once cooking is complete, release pressure using the natural release function for 10 minutes, then release the remaining pressure by using a quick release. (Beans will be very tender and skins loosened.) Reserving 1 cup of the cooking liquid, drain chickpeas, discarding any loose skins.

3. In a food processor or a blender, pulse the garlic, lemon juice, cumin, and salt until the garlic is chopped. Add the tahini and ⅓ cup of the reserved cooking liquid; pulse until smooth. Add the chickpeas and process until smooth, stopping and stirring occasionally. Store in an airtight container in the refrigerator up to two weeks. Makes 4 cups.

EACH TABLESPOON: About 35 calories, 1g protein, 4g carbohydrates, 2g fat (0g saturated), 1g fiber, 40mg sodium.

FUN FLAVORS

Cardamom-Ginger

Stir in **1 tablespoon fresh ginger**, grated and peeled, and **½ teaspoon ground cardamom**.

EACH TABLESPOON: About 35 calories, 1g protein, 4g carbohydrates, 2g fat (0g saturated), 1g fiber, 40mg sodium.

Roasted Pepper & Mint

Finely chop **¾ cup each packed fresh mint and roasted red peppers** with **2 tablespoons capers**; stir into the hummus.

EACH TABLESPOON: About 35 calories, 2g protein, 4g carbohydrates, 2g fat (0g saturated), 1g fiber, 52mg sodium.

TIP

Puree the beans while they are warm for the smoothest results.

Big-Batch Tomato Sauce

Our zesty tomato sauce recipe gives you old-world, slow-simmered flavor in only 20 minutes. Plus, the large quantity offers generous leftovers to pack and freeze for last-minute meals.

PREP: 20 MINUTES   TOTAL: 55 MINUTES

6 ounces thick-cut pancetta or bacon, chopped

1 large red onion, chopped

3 cans (28 ounces each) whole tomatoes in puree

3 tablespoons tomato paste

2 cloves garlic, crushed with a garlic press

2 bay leaves

2 teaspoons dried oregano

¼ teaspoon crushed red pepper

½ teaspoon kosher salt

1. In the Instant Pot, using the sauté function, heat the pot for 1 to 2 minutes. Add the pancetta and onion and cook, uncovered, for 6 minutes, or until the onions are softening. Scrape the bottom of the pot to release any browned bits. Stir in the tomatoes, tomato paste, garlic, bay leaves, oregano, and crushed red pepper. Break up the tomatoes with an immersion blender or potato masher. The tomato pieces should be well crushed.

2. Cover and lock the lid. Select Manual/Pressure Cook and cook at high pressure for 20 minutes. Once cooking is complete, release the pressure by using a quick release. For a smoother sauce, use an immersion blender and blend to the desired consistency. Freeze the sauce for up to 6 months. Makes 10 cups.

EACH CUP: About 115 calories, 5g protein, 12g carbohydrates, 5g fat (2g saturated), 2g fiber, 925mg sodium.

Vegetarian Big-Batch Tomato Sauce

Replace the pancetta with **3 tablespoons olive oil**. Heat over medium heat and add **2 carrots**, chopped, and **1 rib celery**, chopped, along with the onions and seasonings. Increase the tomato paste to **5 tablespoons tomato paste**. Proceed as directed.

EACH CUP: About 105 calories, 3g protein, 14g carbohydrates, 4g fat (1g saturated), 3g fiber, 114mg sodium.

TIP

Serve the sauce over cooked pasta, vegetable noodles, chicken, or pork. Garnish with Pecorino Romano cheese.

TUSCAN VEGGIE STEW
(PAGE 53)

2 | Soups, Stews & Chilis

What's more comforting than the aroma of simmering soup or stew? The idea that after a long day you can prep these dishes and still eat at your normal dinnertime! The pressure function makes short work of stewing even the toughest cuts of meat and delivering the most flavorful chicken broth—all in under an hour. So whether you're in the mood for a comforting bowl of creamy Chicken & Bacon Chowder, Hearty Mushroom Barley Soup, or Pasta Fagioli with Sausage, dinnertime is within reach. Looking for something lighter? Spring Minestrone, Lemon-Dill Chicken Meatball Soup, or Tomato Soup with Cupid Croutons fit the bill.

Chicken Broth

Nothing beats the flavor of homemade chicken broth. Plus our recipe has an added bonus: The cooked chicken can be used in casseroles and salads.

PREP: 10 MINUTES   TOTAL: 40 MINUTES, PLUS COOLING

3½ pounds chicken parts (such as wings, backs, legs)

2 carrots, cut into 2-inch pieces

1 stalk celery, cut into 2-inch pieces

1 medium onion, quartered (see Tip)

5 sprigs fresh parsley

1 clove garlic, smashed with side of chef's knife

½ teaspoon dried thyme

1 bay leaf

6 cups water

TIP

There is no need to peel the onion. Leaving the skin on will add a golden color to the chicken broth.

1. In the Instant Pot, combine the chicken, carrots, celery, onion, parsley, garlic, thyme, bay leaf, and water.

2. Cover and lock the lid. Select Manual/Pressure Cook and cook at high pressure for 30 minutes. Once cooking is complete, release the pressure by using the natural release function.

3. Strain the broth through a colander into a large bowl; discard the solids. Strain again through a sieve into containers; cool. Skim and discard fat from the surface. Cover and refrigerate to use within 3 days, or freeze for up to 4 months. Makes 7½ cups.

EACH CUP: About 40 calories, 5g protein, 5g carbohydrates, 0g fat (0g saturated), 0g fiber, 48mg sodium.

Tex-Mex Chicken Soup

For silky-smooth melted cheese, let the soup stand off the heat to stop simmering. After a few minutes, add a touch of lime juice and stir in the cheese gradually; the acid will help keep it creamy.

PREP: 10 MINUTES   TOTAL: 50 MINUTES

1½ pounds skinless, boneless chicken thighs

3 large stalks celery, sliced

3 carrots, sliced

2 poblano peppers, seeded and chopped

1 large onion, chopped

3 cloves garlic, chopped

2 teaspoons ground cumin

2 teaspoons ground coriander

2 cans (15 ounces each) reduced-sodium white kidney (cannellini) beans, rinsed and drained

4 cups lower-sodium chicken broth, homemade (page 37) or store-bought

3 tablespoons fresh lime juice

½ teaspoon kosher salt

6 ounces Monterey Jack cheese, shredded

Chopped avocado, chopped cilantro, light sour cream, and Baked Tortilla Strips (optional), for garnish

1. In the Instant Pot, combine the chicken, celery, carrots, peppers, onion, garlic, cumin, coriander, beans, and broth. Cover and lock the lid. Select Manual/Pressure Cook and cook at high pressure for 5 minutes. Once cooking is complete, release the pressure by using a quick release. Leave the lid off so the soup cools a bit.

2. Remove the chicken and shred or chop it when it's cool enough to handle. Return the chicken to the pot.

3. Add the lime juice and salt to the pot. Gradually stir in the cheese until melted. Serve topped with avocado, cilantro, sour cream, and Baked Tortilla Strips, if desired. Makes 12 cups.

SERVES 6 (without toppings): About 395 calories, 36g protein, 29g carbohydrates, 14g fat (6g saturated), 8g fiber, 793mg sodium.

Baked Tortilla Strips

Preheat the oven to 425°F. Stack **4 small (4-inch) corn tortillas**; thinly slice them into ⅛-inch-wide strips. Arrange the strips in a single layer on a large baking sheet. Spray all over with **nonstick cooking spray** or **oil**. Bake 4 to 5 minutes, or until deep golden brown. Let cool completely.

SERVES 6: About 30 calories, 1g protein, 5g carbohydrates, 1g fat (0g saturated), 1g fiber, 3mg sodium.

> **TIP**
>
> Make tortilla strips in your air fryer! Preheat the air fryer to 350°F. Spray 4 small (4-inch) corn tortillas with cooking spray or oil and stack. Cut the stack into ⅛-inch-wide strips and place them in the air fryer basket. Air-fry 6 minutes, or until deep golden brown, stirring twice. Let cool completely

Lemon-Dill Chicken Meatball Soup

Add a boost of nutrition and color by placing ½ cup torn spinach in the bottom of each bowl before ladling in the hot soup. Serve with lemon wedges.

PREP: 10 MINUTES   TOTAL: 40 MINUTES

1 pound ground chicken or turkey breast

¼ cup finely chopped fresh dill

1 teaspoon grated lemon zest

Kosher salt

Ground black pepper

2 teaspoons olive oil

1 medium onion, chopped

2 stalks celery, sliced

5 cups lower-sodium chicken broth, homemade (page 37) or store-bought

2 cups water

3 carrots, sliced

¾ cups bulgur or cracked wheat

1. In a bowl, combine the ground chicken, dill, lemon zest, 1¼ teaspoon salt, and ¼ teaspoon pepper.

2. In the Instant Pot, using the sauté function, heat the oil for 1 to 2 minutes. Add the onion and celery and cook, uncovered, for 4 minutes, or until softened, stirring occasionally.

3. Add the broth and water to the pot, leaving the sauté function on. Using a 1-inch scoop (or 2 teaspoons), drop the chicken mixture into the pot. Add the carrots, bulgur, 1 teaspoon salt, and ¼ teaspoon pepper to the pot. Hit cancel to turn off the sauté function. Cover and lock the lid. Select Manual/Pressure Cook and cook at high pressure for 4 minutes. Once cooking is complete, release the pressure by using a quick release. Makes 10 cups.

SERVES 4: About 270 calories, 30g protein, 29g carbohydrates, 4g fat (0g saturated), 5g fiber, 1,246mg sodium.

> ### TIP
> To save time bringing large amounts of liquid up to temperature, leave the sauté or Manual/Pressure Cook function on while you are prepping and adding ingredients to the pot.

Chicken & Bacon Chowder

Like most soups and chowders, this one tastes even better the next day. You can substitute a small onion for the shallots.

PREP: 15 MINUTES   TOTAL: 55 MINUTES

4 slices thick-cut bacon, chopped

3 stalks celery, chopped

2 medium shallots, finely chopped

¼ teaspoon cayenne pepper

Kosher salt

1 quart lower-sodium chicken broth, homemade (page 37) or store-bought

1 pound skinless, boneless chicken thighs (about 4 thighs)

1 pound red potatoes, cut into 1-inch chunks

1½ cups whole milk

¼ cup all-purpose flour

2 cups fresh or frozen corn

Thinly sliced fresh basil, for garnish

Oyster crackers, for serving (optional)

1. In the Instant Pot, using the sauté function, cook the bacon, uncovered, for 8 minutes, or until crisp and browned, stirring occasionally. With a slotted spoon, transfer the bacon to a plate; set aside. Pour off all but 1 tablespoon of the bacon fat.

2. Add the celery, shallots, cayenne, and ¼ teaspoon salt. Cook 3 minutes, or until softening, stirring occasionally. Add the broth and stir, scraping the browned bits from the bottom of the pot. Hit cancel to turn off the sauté function.

3. Add the chicken to the pot. Cover and lock the lid. Select Manual/Pressure Cook and cook at high pressure for 5 minutes. Release the pressure by using a quick release. Stir in the potatoes. Cover and lock the lid. Select Manual/Pressure Cook and cook at high pressure for 5 minutes. Once cooking is complete, release the pressure by using a quick release.

4. With tongs, transfer the chicken to a bowl and shred it using two forks. In a small bowl, whisk the milk and flour together until smooth. Select the sauté function and stir in the milk mixture and the corn. Bring to a simmer and cook 5 minutes, or until thickened, stirring occasionally. Stir in the chicken and ¾ teaspoon salt. Garnish with basil and the reserved bacon. Serve with oyster crackers, if desired. Makes 9½ cups.

SERVES 6: About 300 calories, 25g protein, 30g carbohydrates, 9g fat (4g saturated), 3g fiber, 896mg sodium.

Cod & Bacon Chowder

Omit the chicken. Follow steps 1 and 2. Follow step 3 for cooking the potatoes for 5 minutes and release the pressure using a quick release. Select the sauté function and stir in the milk mixture; **corn; 1 pound cod fillet**, cut into 1½-inch pieces; and **¾ teaspoon salt**. Bring to a simmer and cook 3 to 5 minutes, or until the fish is opaque throughout and the chowder thickens, stirring occasionally. Garnish with **basil** and the reserved **bacon**. Serve with **oyster crackers**, if desired. Makes 10 cups.

SERVES 6: About 275 calories, 24g protein, 31g carbohydrates, 7g fat (3g saturated), 3g fiber, 881mg sodium.

Three-Bean Sweet Potato Chili

If you like your chili spicy, leave the seeds and ribs in the chipotle chilies. If not, then remove the seeds and ribs before chopping.

PREP: 20 MINUTES TOTAL: 45 MINUTES

1 tablespoon vegetable oil

1 medium onion, finely chopped

2 chipotle chilies in adobo, chopped

3 cloves garlic, finely chopped

1 tablespoon ground cumin

1 tablespoon chili powder

Kosher salt

1¼ pounds sweet potatoes, peeled and cut into 1-inch chunks

1 can (28 ounces) diced tomatoes

1 can (15 ounces) tomato puree

2 cups frozen shelled edamame, thawed

1 can (14 ounces) reduced-sodium pinto beans, rinsed and drained

1 can (14 ounces) reduced-sodium black beans, rinsed and drained

1 cup water

Shredded Cheddar cheese and sour cream, for garnish (optional)

1. In the Instant Pot, using the sauté function, heat the oil for 1 to 2 minutes. Add the onion and cook, uncovered, for 3 minutes, or until softened, stirring occasionally. Stir in the chipotle chilies, garlic, cumin, chili powder, and ¼ teaspoon salt and cook 1 minute, stirring. Hit cancel to turn off the sauté function.

2. Stir in the sweet potatoes, diced tomatoes, tomato puree, edamame, pinto beans, black beans, and water. Cover and lock the lid. Select Manual/Pressure Cook and cook at high pressure for 10 minutes. Once cooking is complete, release the pressure by using a quick release. Stir in ¾ teaspoon salt.

3. To serve, garnish with Cheddar cheese and sour cream, if desired. Makes 11 cups.

SERVES 6: About 335 calories, 17g protein, 57g carbohydrates, 6g fat (0 saturated), 16g fiber, 942mg sodium.

Spicy Black Bean Soup

For a satisfying meal, serve this hearty soup with
a spinach, orange, and avocado salad.

PREP: 10 MINUTES   TOTAL: 55 MINUTES

1 tablespoon olive oil

1 large onion, chopped

3 cloves garlic, finely chopped

1½ tablespoons chili powder

¼ teaspoon cayenne pepper

2 teaspoons ground cumin

4 cups lower-sodium chicken broth, homemade
(page 37) or store-bought

1 pound dried black beans, picked over
(2½ cups)

1 large red bell pepper, chopped

4 cups water

2 teaspoons kosher salt

⅓ cup coarsely chopped fresh cilantro

Light yogurt, chopped red onion, cilantro, and
lime wedges, for serving

TIP

If you like your soup smooth, spoon one-third
of the mixture into a blender; cover, with
the center part of the lid removed to let
the steam escape, and puree until smooth.
Pour the puree into a bowl. Repeat with the
remaining mixture. (Alternatively, puree the
soup in the pot using an immersion blender.)

1. In the Instant Pot, using the sauté function,
heat the oil for 1 to 2 minutes. Add the onion
and cook, uncovered, for 3 minutes, or until
softening, stirring occasionally. Stir in the garlic,
chili powder, cayenne, and 1½ teaspoons of the
cumin and cook 30 seconds, stirring. Hit cancel
to turn off the sauté function.

2. Add the broth, beans, bell pepper, and water
to the pot. Cover and lock the lid. Select Manual/
Pressure Cook and cook at high pressure for
30 minutes. Once cooking is complete, release
the pressure by using a quick release. Stir in
the salt, cilantro, and the remaining ½ teaspoon
cumin.

3. To serve, top the soup with dollops of yogurt,
red onion, and cilantro. Serve with lime wedges.
Makes 10 cups.

SERVES 6 (without yogurt): About 310 calories,
17g protein, 54g carbohydrates, 4g fat (1g saturated),
14g fiber, 982mg sodium.

Tomato Soup with Cupid Croutons

This simple soup tastes like the canned version we grew up with but better. Adding the bread thickens the soup and gives it a velvety texture.

PREP: 15 MINUTES   **TOTAL:** 30 MINUTES

2 tablespoons olive oil

1 medium onion, chopped

2 cloves garlic, chopped

3 cups lower-sodium vegetable or chicken broth, homemade (page 37) or store-bought

1 can (28 ounces) whole peeled tomatoes

2 bay leaves

1 teaspoon kosher salt

4 slices white bread

1 tablespoon butter

1 teaspoon sugar

¼ teaspoon ground black pepper

1. In the Instant Pot, using the sauté function, heat the oil for 1 to 2 minutes. Add the onion and garlic and cook, uncovered, for 5 minutes, or until golden, stirring occasionally. Hit cancel to turn off sauté function.

2. Add the broth, tomatoes, bay leaves, and salt to the pot. Cover and lock the lid. Select Manual/Pressure Cook and cook at high pressure for 5 minutes. Once cooking is complete, release the pressure by using a quick release.

3. Meanwhile, trim and discard the crusts from the bread. With a heart-shaped cookie cutter, cut 4 hearts from the bread slices; toast the hearts. Remove the bay leaves from the soup and stir in the bread scraps. Stir in the butter and sugar.

4. In a blender or using an immersion blender, blend the soup in batches until smooth. Stir in the pepper. Top the soup with heart croutons and serve. Makes 6 cups.

SERVES 4: About 185 calories, 3g protein, 21g carbohydrates, 10g fat (3g saturated), 3g fiber, 1,084mg sodium.

TIP

Almost any bowl of soup can be enhanced with an added splash of color or a bit of extra flavor. Chopped fresh herbs are the simplest of all garnishes. Choose an herb that complements the soup's flavor and color. For the best results, chop or snip fresh herbs just before using. Pureed soups can also accommodate other kinds of garnishes. The smooth texture of a pureed bean or tomato soup calls out for a sprinkling of freshly grated Parmesan cheese or crumbled bacon. Pureed vegetable soups can also be topped with a drizzle of heavy cream.

Beef Vegetable Soup

In the Instant Pot, beef shanks cook to a tender, melt-in-your-mouth texture. This rich, meaty dish tastes even better after a day or two, so it's a great make-ahead choice.

PREP: 25 MINUTES   TOTAL: 1 HOUR 40 MINUTES

1 tablespoon vegetable oil

1½ pounds bone-in beef shank crosscuts (about 1½ inches thick)

1 medium onion, chopped

1½ cups beef broth

3 cloves garlic, finely chopped

2 large carrots, chopped

1 large stalk celery, chopped

½ small head green cabbage (8 ounces), cored and chopped (4 cups)

4 ounces dried lima beans (about ½ cup)

¾ pound all-purpose potatoes, peeled and cut into 1-inch pieces

1 can (14½ ounces) petite diced tomatoes, drained

¾ teaspoon dried thyme

⅛ teaspoon ground cloves

Kosher salt

4 cups water

½ cup frozen whole kernel corn

½ cup frozen peas

½ teaspoon ground black pepper

¼ cup chopped fresh parsley

1. In the Instant Pot, select the sauté function and adjust the heat to more. Add the oil and heat 2 to 3 minutes. Add the beef shanks; they will overlap. Cook, uncovered, for 10 minutes, or until well browned, turning once. Transfer to a plate.

2. Add the onion to the pot and cook 1 minute, or until slightly softened, stirring occasionally.

Add the broth and stir, scraping up any browned bits on the bottom of the pot. Return the beef to the pot. Hit cancel to turn off the sauté function.

3. Cover and lock the lid. Select Manual/Pressure Cook and cook at high pressure for 20 minutes. Release the pressure by using a quick release. Add the garlic, carrots, celery, cabbage, lima beans, potatoes, tomatoes, thyme, cloves, 1 teaspoon salt, and the water. Cover and lock the lid. Select Manual/Pressure Cook and cook at high pressure for 20 minutes. Once cooking is complete, release the pressure by using the natural release function for 15 minutes, then release the remaining pressure using a quick release. With a slotted spoon, transfer the beef to a cutting board. Cut the beef into ½-inch pieces, discarding any bones and gristle.

4. Select the sauté function and stir in the beef, corn, peas, pepper, and 1 teaspoon salt. Bring to a boil and cook 3 minutes, or until the corn and peas are hot. Sprinkle with parsley and serve. Makes 12 cups.

SERVES 8: About 180 calories, 15g protein, 21g carbohydrates, 4g fat (1g saturated), 4g fiber, 779mg sodium.

TIP

If your produce is going bad, use it in a big batch of soup—when the veggies are cooked, you won't notice that they were a bit past their prime.

Hearty Mushroom Barley Soup

We suggest using a combination of white button mushrooms and cremini mushrooms here, but you can use other varieties such as portobellos (but be sure to scrape away the dark undersides, called the gills). If you're using shiitake mushrooms, trim and discard the tough stems.

PREP: 20 MINUTES   TOTAL: 40 MINUTES

1 tablespoon olive oil

1 medium onion, chopped

1 tablespoon tomato paste

4 cups beef broth

1 pound mushrooms, trimmed and sliced

3 large carrots, halved lengthwise and cut crosswise into ¼-inch-thick slices

3 stalks celery, cut into ¼-inch-thick slices

¾ cup pearl barley

2 tablespoons dry sherry

½ teaspoon kosher salt

2½ cups water

1. In the Instant Pot, using the sauté function, heat the oil for 1 to 2 minutes. Add the onion and cook, uncovered, for 4 minutes, or until the onion begins to brown, stirring occasionally. Stir in the tomato paste. Add the broth, mushrooms, carrots, celery, barley, sherry, salt, and water. Hit cancel to turn off the sauté function.

2. Cover and lock the lid. Select Manual/Pressure Cook and cook at high pressure for 15 minutes. Once cooking is complete, release the pressure by using the natural release function. Makes 10 cups.

SERVES 6: About 160 calories, 7g protein, 28g carbohydrates, 3g fat (0g saturated), 7g fiber, 763mg sodium.

Spring Minestrone

To save more time, start heating the broth on the sauté function while you gather your ingredients. As you chop the vegetables, add them to the pot and then cover, lock the lid, and proceed as directed.

PREP: 12 MINUTES   TOTAL: 45 MINUTES

2 quarts lower-sodium vegetable or chicken broth, homemade (page 37) or store-bought

2 medium carrots, chopped

3 large red potatoes, peeled and cut in ½-inch pieces

1 medium leek, well rinsed and thinly sliced

1 can (15 ounces) reduced-sodium navy beans, rinsed and drained

8 sprigs fresh thyme, tied together

1 bunch asparagus, sliced

2 tablespoons chopped fresh dill

½ teaspoon kosher salt

¼ teaspoon ground black pepper

1 tablespoon olive oil (optional)

1. In the Instant Pot, combine the broth, carrots, potatoes, leek, beans, and thyme. Cover and lock the lid. Select Manual/Pressure Cook and cook at high pressure for 4 minutes. Once cooking is complete, release the pressure by using a quick release.

2. Select the sauté function. Stir in the asparagus and simmer for 3 minutes. Stir in the dill, salt, and pepper. Serve with a drizzle of olive oil, if using. Makes 11 cups.

SERVES 4: About 380 calories, 15g protein, 80g carbohydrates, 1g fat (0g saturated), 14g fiber, 770mg sodium.

Split Pea Soup with Bacon

The amount of liquid needed for bean, pea, and lentil soups can vary, depending on how old and dry the legumes are. If you're enjoying the soup a day or two after cooking it, stir in some water to loosen the thick porridge texture.

PREP: 15 MINUTES   TOTAL: 45 MINUTES

3 slices thick-cut bacon, chopped

2 carrots, peeled and chopped

2 stalks celery, chopped

1 medium onion, chopped

2 large cloves garlic, crushed with a garlic press

1 package (16 ounces) dry split green peas, rinsed and picked over

4 cups lower-sodium chicken broth, homemade (page 37) or store-bought

3 cups water

1 bay leaf

¼ teaspoon ground allspice

1½ teaspoons kosher salt

¼ teaspoon ground black pepper

1. In the Instant Pot, using the sauté function, cook the bacon, uncovered, for 6 minutes, or until crisped, stirring occasionally. With a slotted spoon, transfer the bacon to a plate. Pour off all but 1 tablespoon bacon fat. Add the carrots, celery, and onion to the pot. Cook for 2 minutes, or until softening, stirring to scrape up the browned bits from the bottom of the pot. Add the garlic, peas, broth, water, bay leaf, and allspice. Hit cancel to turn off the sauté function.

2. Cover and lock the lid. Select Manual/Pressure Cook and cook at high pressure for 8 minutes. Release the pressure by using the natural release function for 15 minutes, then release the remaining pressure by using a quick release.

3. Discard the bay leaf. Stir the salt, pepper, and bacon into the soup. Makes 10 cups.

SERVES 6: About 325 calories, 20g protein, 53g carbohydrates, 4g fat (1g saturated), 20g fiber, 859mg sodium.

German Lentil Soup

Prepare as directed but substitute **1 pound lentils**, rinsed and picked over, for the peas, and substitute **¾ teaspoon dried thyme** for the allspice. Makes 10 cups.

SERVES 6: About 310 calories, 22g protein, 49g carbohydrates, 4g fat (1g saturated), 18g fiber, 852mg sodium.

TIP

Instead of tossing away herb stems, veggie peels, or Parmesan rinds, use them to add flavor to homemade stock. It's super simple and tastes better than prepared stock, plus it can be frozen for 4 to 6 months.

Tuscan Veggie Stew

Ladle this hearty soup into bowls and punch up the flavor by topping it with some chopped fresh basil and freshly grated Parmesan. Yum! See photo on page 34.

PREP: 15 MINUTES   TOTAL: 50 MINUTES

1 tablespoon extra-virgin olive oil

1 medium onion, finely chopped

1 bunch Tuscan or curly kale (8 ounces), stemmed and chopped

2 cloves garlic, chopped

6 cups lower-sodium vegetable or chicken broth, homemade (page 37) or store-bought

4 ounces stale bread without crust, torn into small pieces (about 4 cups)

1 pound carrots, chopped

1 can (14 ounces) diced tomatoes

2 cans (14 ounces each) reduced-sodium white kidney (cannellini) beans, rinsed and drained

2 teaspoons cider vinegar

1 cup grated Parmesan cheese, plus more (optional) for garnish

Chopped fresh basil, for garnish

1. In the Instant Pot, using the sauté function, heat the oil for 1 to 2 minutes. Add the onion and cook, uncovered, for 4 minutes, or until softened, stirring occasionally. Add the kale and garlic; cook 4 minutes, until wilted, stirring occasionally. Hit cancel to turn off the sauté function.

2. Add the broth, bread, carrots, tomatoes, and beans to the pot. Cover and lock the lid. Select Manual/Pressure Cook and cook at high pressure for 6 minutes. Once cooking is complete, release the pressure by using a quick release.

3. Stir in the cider vinegar and Parmesan. Garnish with additional Parmesan and chopped basil, if desired. Makes 13 cups.

SERVES 6: About 380 calories, 19g protein, 56g carbohydrates, 9g fat (3g saturated), 13g fiber, 757mg sodium.

Curried Lentil Soup

This gingery soup is a variation on a favorite from the days of the British Raj. Mulligatawny, its traditional name, is the Tamil word for "pepper water."

PREP: 30 MINUTES   TOTAL: 55 MINUTES

2 teaspoons olive oil

1 large onion, finely chopped

2 large stalks celery, finely chopped

1 tablespoon fresh ginger, chopped and peeled

1 large clove garlic, crushed with a press

1 tablespoon curry powder

1 teaspoon ground cumin

1 teaspoon ground coriander

5 cups water

3½ cups lower-sodium vegetable or chicken broth, homemade (page 37) or store-bought

3 large carrots, finely chopped

1 medium Granny Smith apple, peeled, cored, and chopped

1 package (16 ounces) lentils, rinsed and picked over

¼ cup chopped fresh cilantro

1½ teaspoons kosher salt

Plain low-fat yogurt, for serving

1. In the Instant Pot, using the sauté function, heat the oil for 1 to 2 minutes. Add the onion and celery and cook, uncovered, for 4 minutes, or until softened, stirring occasionally. Add the ginger, garlic, curry powder, cumin, and coriander to the pot; cook for 1 minute, stirring occasionally. Hit cancel to turn off the sauté function.

2. Add the water, broth, carrots, apple, and lentils to the pot. Cover and lock the lid. Select Manual/Pressure Cook and cook at high pressure for 10 minutes. Once cooking is complete, release the pressure using the natural release function for 10 minutes, then release the remaining pressure by using a quick release.

3. Stir in the cilantro and salt. To serve, top the soup with dollops of yogurt. Makes 12 cups.

SERVES 5 (without yogurt): About 400 calories, 24g protein, 72g carbohydrates, 3g fat (0g saturated), 14g fiber, 721mg sodium.

Pasta Fagioli with Sausage

Want a vegetarian option? Omit the sausage, use vegetable broth, and add a couple chopped carrots along with the onions and a diced zucchini when you add the pasta and beans.

PREP: 15 MINUTES   TOTAL: 50 MINUTES

1 tablespoon olive oil

1 pound sweet Italian sausage links, casings removed

2 medium onions, chopped

3 cups lower-sodium chicken broth, homemade (page 37) or store-bought

2 cloves garlic, crushed with a garlic press

1 cup water

1 can (28 ounces) plum tomatoes

3 cans (15 ounces each) great northern or white kidney (cannellini) beans, rinsed and drained

4 ounces ditalini or tubetti pasta (¾ cup)

5 ounces fresh spinach, cut into 1-inch-wide strips

Freshly grated Parmesan cheese, for serving (optional)

1. In the Instant Pot, using the sauté function, heat the oil for 1 to 2 minutes. Add the sausage and cook, uncovered, for 6 minutes, or until browned, breaking it up with the side of a spoon. With a slotted spoon, transfer the sausage to a plate.

2. Drain off and discard the drippings in the pot, then add the onions. Cook 3 minutes, or until softening, stirring occasionally. Add the broth, garlic, and water. Stir well to scrape up all browned bits from the bottom of the pot. Hit cancel to turn off the sauté function.

3. Add the tomatoes, breaking them up with the side of a spoon. Cover and lock the lid. Select Manual/Pressure Cook and cook at high pressure for 6 minutes. Release the pressure by using a quick release. Stir in the beans and pasta. Cover and lock the lid. Select Manual/ Pressure Cook and cook at high pressure for 3 minutes. Once cooking is complete, release the pressure by using a quick release.

4. Stir in the sausage and spinach; let stand for a few minutes, until the sausage is hot and the spinach wilts. Serve with Parmesan, if you like. Makes 12 cups.

SERVES 8: About 390 calories, 21g protein, 53g carbohydrates, 11g fat (3g saturated), 10g fiber, 952mg sodium.

LENTIL "BOLOGNESE"
SPAGHETTI (PAGE 64)

3 | Beans & Grains

Trying to eat more plant-based foods? The gingery Winter Squash & Lentil Stew is perfect on a cold night. Serve it with a dollop of Greek yogurt—it will still come in under 400 calories. The protein-packed Lentil "Bolognese" Spaghetti is a delicious cheat on ground beef. Long-cooking grains like wheat berries and wild rice get their cooking time halved in the Instant Pot. Plus, risottos are a dream—no stirring required! Once you've got your risotto formula, the possibilities are grand!

Winter Squash & Lentil Stew

A bowl of this stew warms chilly fingers and toes with seasonal flavors of sweet butternut squash and savory lentils. Seconds, anyone?

PREP: 15 MINUTES   TOTAL: 35 MINUTES

2 medium shallots, thinly sliced

1 tablespoon finely chopped peeled fresh ginger

1 tablespoon vegetable oil

1 teaspoon ground coriander

½ teaspoon ground cardamom

1 small butternut squash, peeled, seeded, and cut into 1½-inch chunks

1 pound green lentils, rinsed and picked over

6 cups chicken or vegetable broth, homemade (page 37) or store-bought

Kosher salt

5 cups packed baby spinach

1 tablespoon apple cider vinegar

½ teaspoon ground black pepper

1. In the Instant Pot, using the sauté function, cook the shallots and ginger in the oil, uncovered, for 5 minutes, or until the shallots are golden, stirring occasionally. Add the coriander and cardamom; cook for 1 minute, stirring. Hit cancel to turn off the sauté function.

2. Add the squash, lentils, broth, and ¼ teaspoon salt to the pot. Cover and lock the lid. Select Manual/Pressure Cook and cook at high pressure for 12 minutes. Once cooking is complete, release the pressure by using a quick release.

3. Stir in the spinach, cider vinegar, ½ teaspoon salt, and the pepper. Makes 12 cups.

SERVES 6: About 325 calories, 19g protein, 57g carbohydrates, 4g fat (0g saturated), 15g fiber, 705mg sodium.

Pesto Risotto

Depending on the rice you use, the risotto may need additional water stirred in at the end. This dish makes a great accompaniment to roasted chicken.

PREP: 15 MINUTES   TOTAL: 40 MINUTES

2 medium shallots, finely chopped (about 2 ounces)

1 tablespoon butter or olive oil

2 cups arborio or carnaroli rice

½ cup dry white wine

1 can (14½ ounces) lower-sodium chicken broth, or 1¾ cups homemade broth (page 37)

½ teaspoon kosher salt

1¾ cups water

1 pound ripe tomatoes, seeded and chopped

⅓ cup freshly grated Parmesan cheese

2 tablespoons prepared pesto

⅛ teaspoon ground black pepper

Fresh basil, for garnish

1. In the Instant Pot, using the sauté function, heat the pot for 1 to 2 minutes. Add the shallots and butter and cook, uncovered, for 3 minutes, or until softened, stirring. Add the rice and cook 2 minutes, or until the grains are opaque, stirring. Add the wine and cook for 1 minute, until absorbed, stirring. Hit cancel to turn off the sauté function.

2. Stir in the broth, salt, and 1½ cups water. Cover and lock the lid. Select Manual/Pressure Cook and cook at high pressure for 6 minutes. Once cooking is complete, release the pressure by using a quick release. Stir in the tomatoes, Parmesan, pesto, pepper, and the remaining ¼ cup water, if needed. Cover and let stand 3 minutes. Garnish with basil. Makes 7 cups.

SERVES 6: About 310 calories, 8g protein, 57g carbohydrates, 6g fat (2g saturated), 4g fiber, 412mg sodium.

Shrimp Risotto

The Instant Pot makes for stress-free risotto. It comes out creamy and delicious and requires minimal stirring and attention.

PREP: 10 MINUTES TOTAL: 30 MINUTES

2 teaspoons olive oil or butter

1 onion, finely chopped

1½ cups arborio rice, carnaroli rice, or medium-grain rice

½ cup dry white wine

3 cups lower-sodium chicken broth, homemade (page 37) or store-bought

½ teaspoon kosher salt

1 pound medium (31 to 35 count) peeled and deveined shrimp

¾ cup frozen baby peas, thawed

1 lemon

¼ cup chopped fresh parsley

TIP

Need to quickly thaw peas? Place them in a strainer and run them under hot tap water.

1. In the Instant Pot, using the sauté function, heat the oil for 1 to 2 minutes. Add the onion and cook, uncovered, for 3 minutes, or until softening. Add the rice and stir frequently for 2 minutes, or until the grains are opaque. Add the wine and cook for 1 minute, or until it's absorbed. Hit cancel to turn off the sauté function.

2. Stir in 2½ cups of the broth and the salt. Cover and lock the lid. Select Manual/Pressure Cook and cook at high pressure for 6 minutes. Once cooking is complete, release the pressure by using a quick release.

3. Select the sauté function. Stir in the shrimp, peas, and the remaining ½ cup broth. Grate 1 teaspoon lemon zest and stir it into the pot. Cook 4 minutes, or until the shrimp are opaque and the rice is tender but firm. Stir in the parsley. Cut the remaining lemon into wedges and serve with the risotto. Makes 7 cups.

SERVES 4: About 400 calories, 23g protein, 68g carbohydrates, 4g fat (2g saturated), 5g fiber, 1,214mg sodium.

Creamy Cornmeal Polenta

Serve this as a side dish, topped with sautéed mushrooms and shallots, or as a base for a saucy main like Pork & Peppers Ragù (page 100). Pour the polenta in a shallow bowl to serve; this allows the dish to cool and thicken.

PREP: 5 MINUTES   TOTAL: 45 MINUTES

1 tablespoon unsalted butter

1 medium shallot, finely chopped

2¾ cups lower-sodium chicken broth, homemade (page 37) or store-bought

¾ cup yellow cornmeal

½ cup grated Parmesan cheese

1. In the Instant Pot, using the sauté function, heat the pot for 1 to 2 minutes. Add the butter and shallot and cook, uncovered, for 1 minute, stirring. Add the broth and cook 8 minutes, or until the broth begins to bubble. Slowly whisk in the cornmeal.

2. Hit cancel to turn off the sauté function. Cover and lock the lid. Select Manual/Pressure Cook and cook at high pressure for 6 minutes. Once cooking is complete, release the pressure using the natural release for 10 minutes, then release the remaining pressure by using a quick release. Uncover and allow the polenta to stand for 5 minutes. Stir in the Parmesan and serve. Makes 3 cups.

SERVES 4: About 160 calories, 5g protein, 21g carbohydrates, 6g fat (3g saturated), 4g fiber, 474mg sodium.

Lentil "Bolognese" Spaghetti

Traditional Bolognese sauce takes hours to simmer, but here the time is reduced greatly with the same results. Replacing part of the ground beef in the traditional recipe with lentils provides leaner and healthier plant-based protein.

PREP: 15 MINUTES   TOTAL: 45 MINUTES

1 tablespoon olive oil

8 ounces ground beef (at least 90% lean)

1 small onion, finely chopped

1 medium carrot, finely chopped

2 tablespoons tomato paste

2 cloves garlic, finely chopped

½ teaspoon dried oregano

¼ teaspoon crushed red pepper

1 teaspoon kosher salt

¼ teaspoon ground black pepper

½ pound button or cremini mushrooms, finely chopped

½ cup dried red lentils, picked over and rinsed

1 cup water

1 can (14½ ounces) whole tomatoes in juice

¾ pound spaghetti

¼ cup toasted pine nuts

Grated Pecorino cheese, for serving (optional)

1. In the Instant Pot, select the sauté function and adjust the heat to more. Add the oil and heat for 1 to 2 minutes. Add the beef, onion, and carrot to the pot; cook, uncovered, for 5 minutes, or until the beef is no longer red, stirring to break up the beef with the side of a spoon. Add the tomato paste, garlic, oregano, crushed red pepper, salt, and pepper; cook 30 seconds, stirring constantly. Hit cancel to turn off the sauté function.

2. Stir in the mushrooms, lentils, and water. Add the tomatoes and their juices, crushing them with your hands. Cover and lock the lid. Select Manual/Pressure Cook and cook at high pressure for 15 minutes. Once cooking is complete, release the pressure by using a quick release function.

3. Meanwhile, cook the pasta as the package directs. Drain and toss it with 3 cups of the sauce. Top with pine nuts and Pecorino before serving, if desired. Reserve the remaining sauce by refrigerating for up to 5 days or freezing for up to 3 months. Makes 4½ cups.

SERVES 6: About 380 calories, 18g protein, 55g carbohydrates, 10g fat (2g saturated), 7g fiber, 291mg sodium.

Wheat Berries with Brown Butter & Pecans

Wheat berries or whole-grain wheat kernels are a tasty, toothsome addition to soups, stews, salads, and casseroles.

PREP: 10 MINUTES   TOTAL: 1 HOUR 30 MINUTES, PLUS SOAKING

1 cup wheat berries

4 cups plus 3 tablespoons water

2 tablespoons butter

1 medium onion, chopped

½ cup pecans, coarsely chopped

½ teaspoon kosher salt

⅛ teaspoon ground black pepper

2 tablespoons chopped fresh parsley

Bulgur with Brown Butter & Pecans

In the Instant Pot, combine **2¼ cups water** and **1½ cups bulgur**. Cover and lock the lid. Select Manual/Pressure Cook and cook at high pressure for 6 minutes. Once the cooking is complete, release the pressure by using the natural release function. Let stand 5 minutes and fluff with fork. Continue with step 2.

SERVES 6: About 225 calories, 5g protein, 30g carbohydrates, 11g fat (3g saturated), 6g fiber, 198mg sodium.

> ## TIP
> Double the wheat berries and water to make an extra batch for later. The cooking time will stay the same. To store them, portion, bag, and refrigerate the wheat berries for up to 5 days or freeze them for up to 4 months.

1. In the Instant Pot, combine the wheat berries and 4 cups water. Cover and lock the lid. Select Manual Pressure/Cook and cook at high pressure for 50 minutes. Once cooking is complete, release the pressure using the natural release function for 10 minutes, then release the remaining pressure by using a quick release. (Wheat berries should be tender but still firm to the bite.) Drain well. Wipe out the pot. (The wheat berries can be cooked ahead and refrigerated for up to 5 days.)

2. Using the sauté function, heat the pot for 1 to 2 minutes. Add the butter and onion and cook, uncovered, for 5 minutes, stirring frequently, until tender. Stir in the pecans, salt, and pepper. Cook, stirring occasionally, until the pecans are lightly toasted and the butter begins to brown, about 2 minutes. Stir in the wheat berries and the remaining 3 tablespoons water. Cook 3 minutes, stirring occasionally, until heated through. Stir in the parsley. Makes 3 cups.

SERVES 6: About 210 calories, 5g protein, 27g carbohydrates, 11g fat (3g saturated), 5g fiber, 235mg sodium.

Wild Rice with Pepitas & Shredded Carrots

With the pressure cooker, this brown- and wild-rice combo
comes out tender and moist but still chewy.

PREP: 10 MINUTES   TOTAL: 40 MINUTES

3 cloves garlic, finely chopped

1 tablespoon olive oil

1 cup long-grain brown rice

½ cup wild rice, rinsed

2¾ cups lower-sodium chicken broth,
homemade (page 37) or store-bought

½ cup shredded carrot

⅓ cup roasted unsalted pepitas (pumpkin
seeds)

1 tablespoon butter

½ teaspoon kosher salt

⅛ teaspoon ground black pepper

1. In the Instant Pot, using the sauté function,
cook the garlic in the oil, uncovered, for
1 minute, stirring. Stir in the brown rice, wild
rice, and broth. Hit cancel to turn off the sauté
function. Cover and lock the lid. Select Manual/
Pressure Cook and cook at high pressure for
25 minutes. Once cooking is complete, release
the pressure by using the natural release
function.

2. Stir in the carrot, pepitas, butter, salt, and
pepper. Makes 5 cups.

SERVES 6: About 260 calories, 7g protein,
40g carbohydrates, 9g fat (2g saturated), 3g fiber,
376mg sodium.

COQ AU VIN (PAGE 75)

4 | Chicken

Chicken doesn't take that long to cook, so why do you need pressure? The Instant Pot helps keep chicken moist and tender. Bye, dry breast meat! Chicken Breasts with Quick Sauces offers seven options for the fastest dinner in the book. Choose from Creamy Mushroom to Apple-Curry to Chinese Ginger to Provençal and find your new favorites. We're also stewing, braising, and sautéing chicken and turning dishes with longer prep times like Chicken Cacciatore, Tikka Masala, and Arroz con Pollo into weeknight staples. With two very delicious exceptions—Coq au Vin and Turkey Thighs, Osso Buco-Style—everything can be on the table in less than an hour, and using boneless cuts halves that time!

Spicy Peanut Chicken

The combination of cumin, cinnamon, cilantro, peanut butter, and tomatoes creates an intriguing sauce for tender chicken. The spice level is mild when using ¼ teaspoon of crushed red pepper; if you like it spicy, use ½ teaspoon. Serve this over brown rice.

PREP: 20 MINUTES   TOTAL: 1 HOUR

1½ teaspoons ground cumin

¼ teaspoon ground cinnamon

4 boneless chicken thighs (1½ pounds), skin and fat removed

4 chicken drumsticks (1 pound), skin and fat removed

1 can (28 ounces) diced tomatoes, drained and juice reserved

¼ cup packed fresh cilantro leaves, plus additional sprigs for garnish

3 cloves garlic, peeled

Kosher salt

¼ to ½ teaspoon crushed red pepper

1 tablespoon vegetable oil

1 medium onion, thinly sliced

¼ cup creamy peanut butter

1. In a small bowl, combine the cumin and cinnamon; pat the chicken dry and sprinkle it with the spice mixture.

2. Measure the reserved tomato juice; if necessary, add enough water to equal 1 cup.

3. In a blender, combine the tomato juice, cilantro leaves, garlic, ½ teaspoon salt, and crushed red pepper. Blend until smooth.

4. In the Instant Pot, using the sauté function, heat the oil for 1 to 2 minutes. Add the onion and cook for 4 minutes, or until golden, stirring occasionally. Add the tomato juice mixture and stir to scrape up any browned bits from the bottom of the pot. Hit cancel to turn off the sauté function.

5. Add the chicken and diced tomatoes to the pot; stir to coat the chicken with the sauce. Cover and lock the lid. Select Manual/Pressure Cook and cook at high pressure for 12 minutes. Once cooking is complete, release the pressure using the natural release function, about 15 minutes.

6. Transfer the chicken to a plate. Pour the sauce into a bowl; skim off and discard any excess fat. In a small bowl, stir ½ cup of the sauce, the peanut butter, and ½ teaspoon salt until smooth. Return the remaining sauce to the Instant Pot and select the sauté function. Stir in the peanut butter mixture and bring the sauce to a boil. Simmer 8 minutes, or until the sauce thickens and is reduced to about 3 cups, stirring frequently to prevent sticking. Hit cancel to turn off the sauté function. Return the chicken to the pot, pressing it into the sauce. Let stand 5 minutes to heat through. Garnish with cilantro sprigs and serve.

SERVES 4: About 390 calories, 39g protein, 17g carbohydrates, 19g fat (4g saturated), 3g fiber, 1,166mg sodium.

Chicken Bouillabaisse

Bouillabaisse is traditionally made with seafood, but it also works well with chicken. Serve this brothy chicken and vegetable stew in shallow soup bowls with toasted crusty bread rubbed with garlic and drizzled with olive oil.

PREP: 20 MINUTES   TOTAL: 55 MINUTES

4 large bone-in chicken thighs (2 pounds), skin and fat removed

Kosher salt

1 tablespoon olive oil

2 large carrots, chopped

1 medium onion, finely chopped

1 large fennel bulb (1¼ pounds), cut into ¼-inch-thick slices

4 cloves garlic, finely chopped

½ teaspoon dried thyme

¼ teaspoon cayenne pepper

1 bay leaf

1 cup lower-sodium chicken broth, homemade (page 37) or store-bought

½ cup dry white wine

2 tablespoons Pernod or anisette (anise-flavored liqueur; optional)

Pinch of saffron threads

1 can (14½ ounces) diced tomatoes

1. Season the chicken with ½ teaspoon of the salt.

2. In the Instant Pot, select the sauté function and adjust the heat to more. Add the oil and heat for 1 to 2 minutes. Add the chicken and cook, uncovered, for 10 minutes, or until browned, turning once. Transfer the chicken to a plate.

3. Add the carrots, onion, and fennel to the pot. Cook 4 minutes, or until softening, stirring to scrape any browned bits from the bottom of the pot. Stir in the garlic, thyme, cayenne, bay leaf, and 1 teaspoon salt; cook for 30 seconds, stirring. Hit cancel to turn off the sauté function.

4. Add the broth, wine, and Pernod, if using, to the pot. Crumble in the saffron and stir to combine. Add the tomatoes and top with the chicken, pushing it down into the vegetables to submerge it. Cover and lock the lid. Select Manual/Pressure Cook and cook at high pressure for 8 minutes. Once cooking is complete, release the pressure by using a quick release. Discard the bay leaf and serve.

SERVES 4: About 300 calories, 30g protein, 23g carbohydrates, 9g fat (2g saturated), 7g fiber, 1,284mg sodium.

Arroz con Pollo

The rice is especially moist and flavorful with the addition of garlic, oregano, and cayenne pepper. You can use chicken drumsticks instead of thighs.

PREP: 15 MINUTES   TOTAL: 50 MINUTES, PLUS STANDING

6 medium bone-in chicken thighs (1½ pounds), skin and fat removed

Kosher salt

¼ teaspoon ground black pepper

1 tablespoon vegetable oil

1 medium onion, finely chopped

1 red bell pepper, coarsely chopped

1 cup long-grain white rice

2 cloves garlic, finely chopped

½ teaspoon dried oregano, crumbled

¼ teaspoon cayenne pepper

1½ cups lower-sodium chicken broth, homemade (page 37) or store-bought

1 cup frozen peas, thawed

¼ cup pimiento-stuffed olives, chopped

¼ cup chopped fresh cilantro

Lemon wedges, for serving

1. Season the chicken with ½ teaspoon salt and the pepper.

2. In the Instant Pot, using the sauté function, heat the oil for 1 to 2 minutes. Cook the chicken in batches, uncovered, for 6 minutes, or until lightly browned, turning once. Transfer the chicken to a plate.

3. To the pot, add the onion and bell pepper; cook 1 minute, stirring the bottom of the pot to scrape up any browned bits. Stir in the rice, garlic, oregano, cayenne, and ½ teaspoon salt and cook for 30 seconds, stirring. Stir in the broth. Hit cancel to turn off the sauté function.

4. Return the chicken to the pot, pushing it down into the rice mixture to submerge it. Cover and lock the lid. Select Manual/Pressure Cook and cook at high pressure for 8 minutes. Once cooking is complete, release the pressure by using a quick release.

5. Remove the lid and sprinkle the peas on top. Replace the lid, keeping slightly ajar, and let everything stand 10 minutes. Remove the chicken and rice to a platter and sprinkle with olives and cilantro; serve with lemon wedges.

SERVES 4: About 400 calories, 27g protein, 51g carbohydrates, 9g fat (2g saturated), 3g fiber, 876mg sodium.

Chicken Coconut Curry

Some herbs and spices can lose their vibrant flavors under pressure. Once this curry is cooked, stir in a little extra spice for an additional flavor boost. See photo on page 2.

PREP: 15 MINUTES   TOTAL: 35 MINUTES

1 (2-inch) piece peeled fresh ginger

1 teaspoon olive oil

1 large onion, chopped

4 cloves garlic, chopped

1 red chili, seeded and finely chopped, or ¼ teaspoon crushed red pepper

2 pounds boneless, skinless chicken breasts, halved lengthwise and sliced crosswise

1 can (28 ounces) crushed tomatoes

1 cup coconut milk

1 teaspoon kosher salt

1 tablespoon plus ½ teaspoon garam masala

2 tablespoons cornstarch dissolved in 3 tablespoons water

Rice, cilantro, chopped cashews, and sliced red chilies (optional), for serving

1. Grate 1½ teaspoons ginger; chop the remaining ginger and keep it separate. In the Instant Pot, using the sauté function, heat the oil for 1 to 2 minutes. Add the onion to the pot, and cook, uncovered, for 4 minutes or until softening, stirring occasionally. Stir in the garlic, chili, and chopped ginger; cook 30 seconds. Stir in the chicken, tomatoes, coconut milk, salt, and 1 tablespoon of the garam masala, scraping the bottom of the pot to remove any browned bits. Hit cancel to turn off the sauté function.

2. Cover and lock the lid. Select Manual/Pressure Cook and cook at high pressure for 4 minutes. Release the pressure by using a quick release.

3. Select the sauté function. Stir the cornstarch mixture and gradually add it to the pot, stirring. Add the grated ginger and the remaining ½ teaspoon garam masala. Cook 1 to 2 minutes, or until thickened. Serve over rice, topped with cilantro, cashews, and chilies, if desired.

SERVES 6: About 335 calories, 38g protein, 18g carbohydrates, 13g fat (8g saturated), 4g fiber, 642mg sodium.

Coq au Vin

The time taken here to build up flavor is well worth it. Once the pot is up to pressure, this tasty dish cooks in a record 8 minutes. Basic Mashed Potatoes (page 24) are the perfect base for this classic dish. See photo on page 68.

PREP: 30 MINUTES   TOTAL: 1 HOUR 25 MINUTES

12 sprigs fresh parsley

2 bay leaves

Cooking spray

4 slices bacon, cut into ¾-inch pieces

3 pounds assorted skinless chicken pieces

Kosher salt

Ground black pepper

2 tablespoons tomato paste

1 small onion, chopped

1 carrot, chopped

½ celery stalk, chopped

1½ cups dry red wine

1 cup lower-sodium chicken broth, homemade (page 37) or store-bought

10 ounces mushrooms, trimmed and halved

18 pearl onions (generous 1 cup), peeled (10-ounce package)

2½ tablespoons all-purpose flour

⅓ cup water

2 tablespoons chopped fresh parsley

1. With string, tie together the parsley sprigs and bay leaves.

2. In the Instant Pot, using the sauté function, heat the pot for 1 to 2 minutes. Coat the bottom of the insert with cooking spray. Add the bacon and cook, uncovered, for 5 minutes or until crisp. With a slotted spoon, transfer it to paper towels to drain. Sprinkle the chicken with ½ teaspoon salt and ¼ teaspoon pepper. Add the chicken to the pot, in batches, and cook until golden brown, about 8 minutes. Transfer the browned chicken pieces to a bowl.

3. Stir in the tomato paste, onion, carrot, and celery; add the wine. Hit cancel; reselect the sauté function and adjust the heat to more. Heat to boiling and cook 5 minutes, scraping to release any browned bits on the bottom of the pot. Add the broth, chicken, mushrooms, parsley bundle, and about half of the bacon to pot. Place the pearl onions on top.

4. Cover and lock the lid. Select Manual/Pressure Cook and cook at high pressure for 8 minutes. Once cooking is complete, release the pressure by using the natural release function for 10 minutes, then release the remaining pressure by using a quick release. Hit cancel, and select the sauté and more functions.

5. Remove the chicken, mushrooms, and onions with a slotted spoon and place them in a serving dish. Skim and discard the excess fat from the pot. Once the mixture is simmering, cook 7 minutes. Meanwhile, whisk together the flour and water. Gradually whisk this mixture into the pot and cook 3 minutes, or until thickened. Spoon over the chicken and top with chopped parsley. Crumble the remaining bacon on top.

SERVES 6: About 280 calories, 32g protein, 16g carbohydrates, 9g fat (3g saturated), 1g fiber, 462mg sodium.

Chicken Cacciatore

This tender chicken leg is completely infused with Italian herbs and flavors.

PREP: 10 MINUTES   TOTAL: 35 MINUTES

1 package (8 ounces) sliced cremini mushrooms

1 tablespoon olive oil

1 medium onion, thinly sliced

3 cloves garlic, thinly sliced

2 tablespoons all-purpose flour

1 can (28 ounces) diced tomatoes

1¼ teaspoons dried oregano

¼ teaspoon salt

¼ teaspoon crushed red pepper flakes

4 bone-in, skinless chicken thighs (about 8 ounces each)

1 medium yellow or green bell pepper, thinly sliced

3 tablespoons chopped fresh basil or parsley

1 teaspoon balsamic vinegar

Freshly grated Parmesan cheese, for serving

1. In the Instant Pot, select the sauté function and adjust the heat to more. Cook the mushrooms in the oil, uncovered, for 4 minutes. Stir in the onion and garlic; cook 4 minutes, or until the onions soften. Sprinkle in the flour and stir. Add the tomatoes, oregano, salt, and red pepper flakes. Stir and scrape up any browned bits from the bottom of the pan.

2. Add the chicken thighs, pressing into the sauce. Cover and lock the lid. Select Manual/Pressure Cook and cook at high pressure for 9 minutes. Once cooking is complete, release the pressure by using a quick release. Transfer the chicken to the plate. Stir and scrape any browned bits off the bottom of the pan if needed.

3. Choose the sauté function and adjust the heat to more. Stir in the bell pepper and cook 4 minutes, or until the peppers are just tender. Stir in the basil and balsamic vinegar. Serve with grated Parmesan.

SERVES 4: About 295 calories, 31g protein, 21g carbohydrates, 9g fat (2g saturated), 3g fiber, 724mg sodium.

TIP

This dish is great served over Creamy Cornmeal Polenta (see page 63).

Turkish Chicken in Walnut Sauce

Forgot to thaw frozen chicken? You can cook individually frozen pieces in the same time with the Instant Pot! Just remember that the time needed for coming up to pressure will be a little longer as the meat defrosts.

PREP: 5 MINUTES   TOTAL: 20 MINUTES

2 cups water

2 bay leaves

6 small skinless, boneless chicken breast halves (1¾ pounds)

Kosher salt

1¼ cups toasted walnuts

3 slices firm white bread, torn into pieces

1 cup lower-sodium chicken broth, homemade (page 37) or store-bought

1 clove garlic, minced

½ teaspoon paprika

⅓ teaspoon cayenne pepper

1. Place the steamer rack in the Instant Pot. Add the water and bay leaves to the pot. Arrange the chicken breasts on the rack and season with ¼ teaspoon salt.

2. Cover and lock the lid. Select Manual/Pressure Cook and cook at high pressure for 00 minutes. Once cooking is complete, release the pressure by using a quick release. Leave the chicken in the pot and check it for doneness using an instant read thermometer; the internal temperature should be 165°F. If the chicken is not to temperature, cover the pot with the heat off and let it stand 5 minutes.

3. Meanwhile, in a food processor with the knife blade attached, process the walnuts and bread pieces until finely ground. Add the broth, garlic, paprika, cayenne, and ¾ teaspoon salt; process until well combined. Set aside.

4. Chop the poached chicken breasts, place them in a medium bowl, and stir half of the walnut sauce into the chicken until combined. Spoon the chicken onto a serving platter and pour the remaining sauce on top. Cover with plastic wrap and let stand 30 minutes or refrigerate up to 8 hours.

SERVES 6: About 330 calories, 34g protein, 9g carbohydrates, 18g fat (2g saturated), 2g fiber, 576mg sodium.

> ### TIP
> Most bulk-packaged chicken breasts weigh 12 to 14 ounces each. If you want to use these, pressure-cook three breasts as directed in the recipe, cooking for 9 minutes at full pressure and using a quick release when cooking is complete. Cut them in half and use as directed. If you want a softer-textured chicken for shredding, add 3 minutes to the cooking time.

Mediterranean Chicken

To prevent skinned chicken from sticking to the Instant Pot, coat the bottom of the inner pot with nonstick cooking spray along with the oil in the recipe.

PREP: 20 MINUTES TOTAL: 40 MINUTES

6 sprigs fresh thyme, plus more for garnish

1 lemon

4 bone-in chicken thighs (2¼ pounds), skin and fat removed

¾ teaspoon kosher salt

¼ teaspoon ground black pepper

Cooking spray

1 tablespoon olive oil

1 large onion, cut in half lengthwise and sliced

½ cup dry white wine

1 can (14½ ounces) no-salt-added petite diced tomatoes

½ cup Kalamata olives, pitted and coarsely chopped

1½ tablespoons all-purpose flour dissolved in 3 tablespoons water

½ teaspoon chopped fresh thyme leaves

Lemon wedges, for serving

1. Tie together the sprigs of thyme. Cut three 4 × 1-inch strips of peel from the lemon and thinly slice them crosswise; grate ½ teaspoon lemon rind and set aside. Season the chicken with the salt and pepper.

2. In the Instant Pot, set on the sauté function, spray the bottom of the insert with cooking spray. Add the oil and heat for 3 minutes. Add the chicken and cook, uncovered, for 8 minutes, or until browned, turning once. Using a slotted spoon, transfer the chicken to a plate.

3. Add the onion to the pot. Cook, stirring frequently, for 3 minutes, or until softening, scraping up any browned bits on the bottom of the pot. Add the wine, tomatoes, lemon peel, half of the olives, the thyme bundle, and the chicken thighs and their juices to the pot.

4. Cover and lock the lid. Select Manual/Pressure Cook and cook at high pressure for 6 minutes. Once cooking is complete, release the pressure using the natural release function for 6 minutes, then release the remaining pressure by using a quick release. Unlock the lid and remove the cover. Select the sauté function.

5. Remove the thyme bundle from the pot and push the chicken to one side. Gradually stir in the flour mixture and remaining olives. Add the grated lemon rind and chopped thyme leaves to the pot. Cook for 2 minutes, or until thickened. Garnish with thyme sprigs and serve with lemon wedges.

SERVES 4: About 310 calories, 32g protein, 13g carbohydrates, 14g fat (2g saturated), 3g fiber, 790mg sodium.

TIP

Serve over a blend of cooked orzo and cauliflower rice.

No-Time Tikka Masala

This Indian favorite is on the table in under an hour.

PREP: 15 MINUTES   TOTAL: 35 MINUTES

1 tablespoon vegetable oil

1 medium onion, finely chopped

1 tablespoon grated peeled fresh ginger

3 cloves garlic, crushed with garlic press

1 tablespoon curry powder

1 teaspoon paprika

1½ pounds boneless, skinless chicken thighs, cut into 1 ½-inch chunks

1 cup canned crushed tomatoes

½ cup chicken broth, homemade (page 37) or store-bought

2 teaspoons sugar

¾ teaspoon salt

½ cup half-and-half

1½ teaspoons cornstarch

¼ cup cilantro leaves, chopped

Rice, for serving

1. In the Instant Pot using the sauté function, heat the oil. Add the onion and cook, uncovered, for 4 minutes, or until golden, stirring occasionally. Add the ginger and garlic; cook 1 minute, stirring. Add the curry powder and paprika; cook 30 seconds, stirring. Stir in the chicken, tomatoes, broth, sugar, and salt. Hit cancel to turn off the sauté function.

2. Cover and lock the lid. Select Manual/Pressure Cook and cook at high pressure for 12 minutes. Once cooking is complete, release the pressure by using a quick release.

3. In a cup, mix the half-and-half and cornstarch. Set the pot to the sauté function and bring the chicken to a simmer. Stir in the half-and-half mixture. Simmer 2 minutes, or until thickened, stirring occasionally. Stir in the cilantro. Serve with rice.

SERVES 4 (without rice): About 335 calories, 37g protein, 14g carbohydrates, 14g fat (4g saturated), 3g fiber, 738mg sodium.

Chicken Breasts with Quick Sauces

The pressure cooker keeps chicken breasts tender and juicy. Consider saving the cooking liquid for soups or sauces.

PREP: 5 MINUTES   TOTAL: 20 MINUTES

4 small skinless, boneless chicken breast halves (6 ounces each)

½ teaspoon kosher salt

¼ teaspoon ground black pepper

1 teaspoon vegetable oil

¾ cup water

Your choice of sauce (at right)

1. Sprinkle the chicken breasts on both sides with the salt and pepper.

2. In the Instant Pot, select the sauté function and adjust the heat to more. Spray the bottom of the pot with cooking spray and heat for 3 minutes. Add the oil; when hot, add 2 chicken breasts. Cook 2 minutes on each side, until lightly browned. Transfer to a plate and repeat with remaining 2 breasts. Hit cancel to turn off the sauté function.

3. Place the steamer rack in the pot and add the water. Place the chicken breasts on the rack, overlapping slightly to fit, if needed. Cover and lock the lid. Select Manual/Pressure Cook and cook at high pressure for 2 minutes. Once cooking is complete, release the pressure by using a quick release. Let the chicken rest in the pot, covered, for 1 minute. Check the chicken pieces for doneness using an instant read thermometer; the internal temperature should be 165°F. Transfer the chicken to a platter and keep warm.

4. Spoon your choice of prepared sauce over the chicken.

> **TIP**
>
> Save the flavor-packed cooking liquid from the pressure-cooking process for pan sauces or soups.

Apple-Curry Sauce

In a skillet, heat **2 teaspoons vegetable oil** over medium heat. Add **1 Golden Delicious apple**, peeled, cored, and chopped, and **1 small onion**, chopped. Cook, stirring occasionally, until tender. Stir in **1½ teaspoons curry powder** and **¼ teaspoon kosher salt**; cook, stirring, for 1 minute. Stir in **½ cup mango chutney**, **½ cup frozen peas**, and **½ cup water**. Heat to boiling; boil 1 minute. Spoon over the chicken.

SERVES 4 (with chicken): About 335 calories, 41g protein, 21g carbohydrates, 9g fat (1g saturated), 3g fiber, 553mg sodium.

Black Bean Salsa

In a skillet, combine **1 can (15 to 19 ounces) black beans**, rinsed and drained; **1 jar (10 ounces) thick-and-chunky salsa**; **1 can (8¾ ounces) whole-kernel corn**, drained; **2 tablespoons chopped fresh cilantro**; and **¼ cup water**. Cook over medium heat, stirring, until heated through, about 1 minute. Spoon over the chicken.

SERVES 4 (with chicken): About 355 calories, 45g protein, 28g carbohydrates, 7g fat (1g saturated), 9g fiber, 1,130mg sodium.

Chinese Ginger Sauce

In a skillet, heat **1 teaspoon vegetable oil** over medium heat. Add **1 red bell pepper**, thinly sliced, and cook until tender-crisp. Add **½ cup water**, **2 tablespoons lower-sodium soy sauce**, **2 tablespoons seasoned rice vinegar**, and **1 tablespoon grated peeled fresh ginger**. Raise the heat to high and bring to a boil; boil 1 minute. Sprinkle with **2 chopped green onions**. Spoon over the chicken.

SERVES 4 (with chicken): About 255 calories, 39g protein, 6g carbohydrates, 7g fat (1g saturated), 1g fiber, 967mg sodium.

Provençal Sauce

In a skillet, heat **1 teaspoon olive or vegetable oil** over medium heat. Add **1 medium onion**, chopped, and cook, stirring, until tender. Stir in **1 can (14½ ounces) Italian-style stewed tomatoes**; **½ cup pitted ripe olives**, each cut in half; **1 tablespoon drained capers**; and **¼ cup water**. Cook, stirring, until heated through, about 1 minute. Spoon over the chicken.

SERVES 4 (with chicken): About 305 calories, 39g protein, 11g carbohydrates, 11g fat (2g saturated), 1g fiber, 827mg sodium.

Creamy Mushroom Sauce

In a skillet, heat **1 teaspoon vegetable oil** over medium heat. Add **10 ounces mushrooms**, trimmed and sliced; **1 medium onion**, thinly sliced; and **¾ teaspoon kosher salt**. Cook, stirring occasionally, until vegetables are golden brown and tender. Reduce the heat to low; stir in **½ cup light sour cream** and **¼ cup water**; heat through—do not boil. Spoon over the chicken.

SERVES 4 (with chicken): About 295 calories, 42g protein, 7g carbohydrates, 10g fat (3g saturated), 1g fiber, 707mg sodium.

Dijon Sauce

In a skillet over low heat, combine **½ cup half-and-half or light cream**, **2 tablespoons Dijon mustard with seeds**, and **¾ cup seedless red or green grapes**, each cut in half. Cook, stirring to blend the flavors, until the sauce has thickened, about 1 minute. Spoon over the chicken.

SERVES 4 (with chicken): About 280 calories, 40g protein, 7g carbohydrates, 9g fat (3g saturated), 0g fiber, 515mg sodium.

Cucumber Raita

Peel, seed, and coarsely shred **1 medium cucumber**. Squeeze out as much liquid as possible. In a small bowl, combine the shredded cucumber with **1 cup (8 ounces) plain yogurt**. Season with **kosher salt and ground black pepper**. Add **1 tablespoon chopped fresh mint**, if you like.

SERVES 4 (with chicken): About 260 calories, 41g protein, 4g carbohydrates, 8g fat (2g saturated), 0g fiber, 406mg sodium.

Red-Cooked Turkey Thighs with Leeks

This often overlooked poultry part is a perfect choice for the Instant Pot, cooking in under 30 minutes. If you're using frozen meat, add 10 minutes to the cook time.

PREP: 10 MINUTES   TOTAL: 50 MINUTES

4 large leeks

½ cup dry sherry

⅓ cup lower-sodium soy sauce

¼ cup packed brown sugar

2 tablespoons minced peeled fresh ginger

3 cloves garlic, crushed with a garlic press

1 teaspoon Chinese five-spice powder

3 small turkey thighs (about 1 pound each), skin removed

2 cups (about half a 16-ounce bag) peeled baby carrots

1½ teaspoons cornstarch dissolved in 1 tablespoon water

1. Cut off the roots and dark-green tops from the leeks. Discard the tough outer leaves. Cut each leek lengthwise in half, then crosswise in half. Rinse the leeks in a large bowl of cold water, swishing to remove any sand. Transfer the leeks to a colander. Repeat, if needed, until no sand remains. Drain well.

2. In the Instant Pot, combine the sherry, soy sauce, brown sugar, ginger, garlic, and five-spice powder. Add the turkey thighs, tossing to coat in the liquid. Cover and lock the lid. Select Manual/Pressure Cook and cook at high pressure for 25 minutes. Once cooking is complete, release the pressure by using a quick release.

3. Add the carrots and leeks to pot. Cover and lock the lid. Select Manual/Pressure Cook and cook at high pressure for 3 minutes. Once cooking is complete, release the pressure by using a quick release.

4. Transfer the turkey and vegetables to a deep platter and cover with foil to keep warm. Select the sauté function and adjust the heat setting to more. Bring to a boil and cook 8 minutes, or until reduced to 1¼ cups, skimming and discarding any fat as it cooks. Add the stirred cornstarch mixture and cook 1 minute, or until thickened. Remove and discard the bones; slice the turkey. Spoon the cooking liquid over the turkey and vegetables.

SERVES 6: About 355 calories, 41g protein, 24g carbohydrates, 10g fat (3g saturated), 2g fiber, 1,005mg sodium.

TIP

You may substitute 1 large onion, peeled and cut into 8 wedges (left attached at the root end) in place of leeks.

Turkey Thighs, Osso Buco–Style

The classic osso buco recipe uses veal shanks, which are expensive and sometimes hard to find, so we adapted the recipe to use turkey thighs. The traditional topping, called gremolata, is a mixture of chopped parsley, garlic, and lemon zest, which adds a bright touch.

PREP: 15 MINUTES   TOTAL: 1 HOUR 30 MINUTES

2 turkey thighs (1¼ pounds each),
  skin removed

Kosher salt

¼ teaspoon ground black pepper

1 tablespoon vegetable oil

1 large onion, chopped

4 carrots, cut into ¾-inch pieces

2 stalks celery, cut into ½-inch pieces

4 cloves garlic, finely chopped

1 can (14½ ounces) whole tomatoes

½ cup dry red wine

1 bay leaf

½ teaspoon dried thyme

1. Sprinkle the turkey with ½ teaspoon salt and the pepper.

2. In the Instant Pot, select the sauté function and adjust the heat to more. Add the oil and heat for 1 to 2 minutes. Add the turkey thighs, one at a time, and cook, uncovered, for 8 minutes, or until browned, turning once. Transfer to a plate.

3. Pour off all but 1 tablespoon of the drippings and add the onion. Cook 5 minutes, stirring to scrape up any browned bits from the bottom of the pot. Add the carrots, celery, and garlic; cook 2 minutes, stirring occasionally. Stir in the tomatoes, wine, bay leaf, and thyme; break up the tomatoes with the side of a spoon. Hit cancel to turn off the sauté function.

4. Return the turkey thighs to the pot, pressing them into the sauce and spooning some vegetables over the top. Cover and lock the lid. Select Manual/Pressure Cook and cook at high pressure for 35 minutes. Once cooking is complete, release the pressure by using the natural release function for 10 minutes, then release the remaining pressure by using a quick release. Transfer the turkey to a cutting board.

5. Discard the bay leaf and stir ¾ teaspoon salt into the sauce. Select the sauté function and cook the sauce for 4 minutes, or until slightly reduced. Hit cancel to turn off the sauté function. Remove the turkey meat from the bones and cut it into bite-size pieces. Gently stir the turkey into the sauce and let stand 5 minutes.

SERVES 4: About 360 calories, 45g protein, 16g carbohydrates, 13g fat (3g saturated), 4g fiber, 1,609mg sodium.

CHILI-BRAISED BEEF
(PAGE 90)

5 | Meat

Performance under pressure—deliciously tender braised meat in half the time. Yes, we're talking pot roast, brisket, pork shoulder, and ribs! Feel like something light? Try Vietnamese-inspired Soy-Braised Beef & Tomato-Mint Salad. Our meaty chilis include a super-easy riff on mole and a hearty braise done Cincinnati-style with some cinnamon to balance the heat. There's cassoulet, Ropa Vieja, Meatball Stroganoff, Boeuf Bourguignon, goulash, and even some pulled pork. If all of these sound too delicious to be low-calorie, they're not. They all come in at under 400 calories a serving, and a few are even under 300, leaving you some calories for bread, rice, or tortillas to mop up the sauce!

Soy-Braised Beef & Tomato-Mint Salad

Serve this saucy mixture over rice or a combination of brown rice noodles and vegetable noodles for a healthy bowl dinner.

PREP: 10 MINUTES   TOTAL: 6 HOURS

5 cloves garlic, smashed

¼ cup packed brown sugar

¼ cup rice or apple cider vinegar

¼ cup lower-sodium soy sauce

3 tablespoons fish sauce

½ teaspoon ground black pepper

3 pounds beef brisket, trimmed of excess fat and cut into 1-inch chunks

1 pint grape tomatoes, cut into halves

1 small red onion, thinly sliced

½ cup fresh mint leaves

1. In the Instant Pot, combine the garlic, brown sugar, cider vinegar, soy sauce, fish sauce, and pepper. Toss in the brisket pieces; press them down with the back of a spoon to submerge. Cover and lock the lid. Select Manual/Pressure Cook and cook at high pressure for 45 minutes. Once cooking is complete, release the pressure by using the natural release function for 10 minutes, then release the remaining pressure using a quick release.

2. Toss the beef with the tomatoes, red onion, and mint leaves.

SERVES 6: About 290 calories, 42g protein, 9g carbohydrates, 10g fat (4g saturated), 2g fiber, 510mg sodium.

Chili-Braised Beef

You can serve this beef in a multitude of ways! Our favorites include over rice or pasta, in tacos, or on rolls. See photo on page 86.

PREP: 15 MINUTES   TOTAL: 1 HOUR 40 MINUTES

2½ pounds beef chuck roast, trimmed and cut into 2-inch chunks

Kosher salt

1 tablespoon vegetable oil

1 large onion (12 ounces), coarsely chopped

4 large cloves garlic, chopped

1 tablespoon smoked paprika

1 tablespoon ancho chili powder

2 teaspoons chipotle chili powder

½ teaspoon ground cinnamon

½ teaspoon ground black pepper

¼ cup tomato paste

1 ¼ cups lower-sodium beef broth

1 tablespoon molasses

Fresh parsley leaves and thinly sliced green onions, for garnish

1. Season the beef with ½ teaspoon salt.

2. In the Instant Pot, using the sauté function, heat the oil for 1 to 2 minutes. Add the onion and ½ teaspoon salt and cook 5 minutes, until golden, stirring occasionally. Stir in the garlic, paprika, both chili powders, the cinnamon, pepper, and ½ teaspoon salt. Stir in the tomato paste. Hit cancel to turn off the sauté function. Add the broth, stirring to scrape up any browned bits from the bottom of the pot.

3. Stir in the beef. Cover and lock the lid. Select Manual/Pressure Cook and cook at high pressure for 50 minutes. Release the pressure by using the natural release function.

4. Using a slotted spoon, transfer the beef and onions to a plate. Pour the cooking liquid into a bowl and skim off any excess fat. Return the cooking liquid to the pot. Select the sauté function and bring the sauce to a boil. Cook 12 minutes, or until reduced to about 2½ cups. Hit cancel to turn off the sauté function. Stir in the molasses.

5. With two forks, shred the beef, discarding any fat. Return the beef to the pot and stir to combine with the sauce. Serve garnished with parsley leaves and sliced green onions.

SERVES 8: About 230 calories, 29g protein, 9g carbohydrates, 8g fat (2g saturated), 2g fiber, 530mg sodium.

Mole Chili con Carne

For convenience, we use canned beans in this recipe. If time allows, cook a batch of dried beans to use instead—you'll discover Instant Pot–cooked beans are creamier and more flavorful than canned and well worth the minimal effort involved.

PREP: 15 MINUTES   TOTAL: 45 MINUTES

1 tablespoon olive oil

2 large onions, chopped

1½ pounds boneless pork shoulder (Boston butt), trimmed and cut into 1-inch pieces

1½ pounds boneless beef chuck, trimmed and cut into 1-inch pieces

1 can (28 ounces) diced tomatoes

4 cloves garlic, chopped

1 tablespoon ground coriander

1 tablespoon ground cumin

1 tablespoon mild paprika

2 teaspoons chipotle chili powder

½ teaspoon ground cinnamon

2 squares (1 ounce each) unsweetened chocolate, chopped

2½ teaspoons kosher salt

3 cans (15 to 19 ounces each) lower-sodium pink beans, red kidney beans, or a combination, rinsed and drained

Warm corn tortillas, for serving (optional)

1. In the Instant Pot, using the sauté function, heat the oil for 1 to 2 minutes. Add the onion and cook 4 minutes, or until softening. Hit cancel to turn off the sauté function. Add the pork, beef, tomatoes, garlic, coriander, cumin, paprika, chili powder, cinnamon, chocolate, and salt. Stir to combine and press the meat down to submerge it.

2. Cover and lock the lid. Select Manual/Pressure Cook and cook at high pressure for 16 minutes. Once cooking is complete, release the pressure by using the natural release for 10 minutes, then release the remaining pressure by using a quick release. Skim off and discard any fat. Select the keep warm feature. Stir in the beans, cover, and let stand 5 minutes, or until the beans are heated through. Spoon the chili into bowls and serve with tortillas, if you like.

SERVES 10: About 385 calories, 33g protein, 33g carbohydrates, 13g fat (5g saturated), 7g fiber, 803mg sodium.

TIP

Whip up dried beans for chilis and soups in less than 10 minutes! In the Instant Pot, combine **1 bag (16 ounces) pink, kidney, or other desired beans**; **1 onion**, peeled and halved; **1 bay leaf**; and **6 cups water**. Cover and lock lid. Select Manual/Pressure Cook and cook at high pressure for 7 minutes. Once cooking is complete, release the pressure by using a quick release. Drain the beans, reserving the liquid if desired. Beans can be refrigerated up to 5 days or frozen up to 3 months.

Latin-Style Beef (Ropa Vieja)

Cutting the brisket into smaller pieces will speed up the cooking process, saving you time and energy, as shredding will be easier.

PREP: 20 MINUTES   TOTAL: 2 HOURS 15 MINUTES

2 teaspoons olive oil

2 large red, yellow, and/or green bell peppers, sliced

1½ tablespoons capers, drained and chopped if large

1 can (14½ ounces) petite diced tomatoes

1 medium onion, chopped

3 cloves garlic, sliced

2 large pickled jalapeño chilies, sliced

1 tablespoon ground cumin

½ teaspoon ground cinnamon

1 teaspoon kosher salt

¼ cup water

1 fresh beef brisket (about 3 pounds), cut into 5-inch chunks

Warm flour or corn tortillas and/or cooked white rice with parsley, for serving (optional)

TIP

For added flavor toss in a few green olives along with the capers in Step 1.

1. In the Instant Pot, select the sauté function and adjust the heat to more. Heat the oil for 1 to 2 minutes. Add the bell peppers and cook 10 minutes, or until almost tender, stirring occasionally. With a slotted spoon, remove the peppers to a bowl, and add the capers. Hit cancel to turn off the sauté function.

2. Add the tomatoes with their juices, the onion, garlic, jalapeños, cumin, cinnamon, salt, and water to the pot. Stir together to combine. Add the brisket, pressing down to submerge.

3. Cover and lock the lid. Select Manual/Pressure Cook and cook at high pressure for 1 hour 10 minutes. Once cooking is complete, release the pressure by using the natural release function for 15 minutes, then release the remaining pressure by using a quick release. Using a slotted spoon, transfer the brisket to a cutting board.

4. Select the sauté function and adjust the heat to more. Simmer the liquid for 15 minutes to reduce it slightly, to about 3½ cups. Skim and discard any fat. With two forks, shred the brisket along the grain into fine strips. Return the brisket and bell peppers to the pot and stir to combine. Cook for 3 minutes, or until heated through. Serve the brisket mixture with tortillas and/or rice, if you like.

SERVES 8: About 290 calories, 37g protein, 7g carbohydrates, 12g fat (4g saturated), 2g fiber, 497mg sodium.

Meatball Stroganoff

Serve these tender meatballs in a creamy sauce over
egg noodles for a classic comfort meal.

PREP: 25 MINUTES   TOTAL: 1 HOUR

1½ pounds lean ground beef (90%)

¾ cup plain dried bread crumbs

1 large egg

¼ cup water

3 garlic cloves, separated, crushed through
  a garlic press

Kosher salt

Ground black pepper

1 tablespoon salted butter

1 medium onion, chopped

1 teaspoon paprika

1½ cups lower-sodium beef broth

1 tablespoon Dijon mustard

1 tablespoon Worcestershire sauce

¾ pound cremini mushrooms, sliced

½ cup sour cream

2 tablespoons all-purpose flour

1. In a large bowl, combine the beef, bread crumbs, egg, water, 1 clove of the garlic, 1 teaspoon salt, and ¼ teaspoon pepper. Mix until blended but not overworked. Using a rounded tablespoon, shape the mixture into 1½-inch meatballs, making 24 meatballs.

2. In the Instant Pot, using the sauté function, heat the pot for 1 to 2 minutes. Add the butter and onion and cook 4 minutes, or until softened, stirring occasionally. Hit cancel to turn off the sauté function. Stir in the paprika and remaining 2 cloves garlic. Add the broth, mustard, and Worcestershire sauce, stirring to scrape any browned bits from the bottom of the pot. Stir in the mushrooms. Add the meatballs to the pot. Cover and lock the lid. Select Manual/Pressure Cook and cook on high pressure for 8 minutes. Release the pressure by using a quick release. Using a slotted spoon, transfer the meatballs to a plate.

3. Select the sauté function and bring the liquid in the pot to a boil. In a small bowl, whisk together the sour cream and flour until smooth. Stir the mixture into the pot and simmer for 2 minutes, or until thickened, stirring frequently. Stir in ½ teaspoon salt and ¼ teaspoon pepper. Hit cancel to turn off the sauté function. Return the meatballs to the pot and let stand 5 minutes to heat through.

SERVES 6: About 355 calories, 29g protein, 18g carbohydrates, 18g fat (8g saturated), 2g fiber, 886mg sodium.

Boeuf Bourguignon

This French stew flavored with wine is delicious served over egg noodles and tastes even better the next day.

PREP: 25 MINUTES   TOTAL: 1 HOUR 50 MINUTES

2 slices thick-cut bacon, chopped

½ pound frozen pearl onions

1 pound mushrooms, such as white button or cremini, cut into halves or quarters if large

2 pounds lean boneless beef chuck, trimmed and cut into 1½-inch pieces

1 medium onion, chopped

2 carrots, peeled and chopped

3 large cloves garlic, finely chopped

1 tablespoon tomato paste

2 cups dry red wine, such as Pinot Noir

3 sprigs fresh thyme

1 bay leaf

2 tablespoons butter, softened

2 tablespoons all-purpose flour

¼ teaspoon ground black pepper

¾ teaspoon kosher salt

1. In the Instant Pot, using the sauté function, cook the bacon for 6 minutes, or until browned, stirring occasionally. Remove to a plate. Pour the bacon fat into a cup and reserve.

2. Return 1 teaspoon of the bacon fat to the pot and add the pearl onions. Cook 3 minutes, or until thawed. Transfer the onions to a large plate. Return 1 more teaspoon of the bacon fat to the pot and add the mushrooms; cook 5 minutes, or until lightly browned, stirring occasionally. Transfer the mushrooms to the plate with the onions.

3. Return the remaining bacon fat to the pot and add half of the beef. Cook 5 minutes, or until browned, turning once. Stir in the chopped onion, carrots, garlic, and tomato paste. Add the wine, stirring to scrape any browned bits from the pot. Stir in the thyme, bay leaf, and remaining beef. Hit cancel to turn off the sauté function.

4. Cover and lock the lid. Select Manual/Pressure Cook and cook at high pressure for 35 minutes. Once cooking is complete, release the pressure by using the natural release function for 20 minutes, then release the remaining pressure by using a quick release.

5. Discard the thyme sprigs and bay leaf. With a slotted spoon, transfer the beef and vegetables to a bowl. Cover to keep warm. Skim off any excess fat from the sauce.

6. Select the sauté function and bring the sauce to a simmer. Stir in the reserved pearl onions and mushrooms; simmer for 10 minutes to reduce the sauce.

7. Mix the butter and flour together until smooth. Stir it into the sauce. Add the pepper, salt, and reserved bacon; simmer for 2 minutes, or until thickened. Hit cancel to turn off the sauté function. Stir in the beef and vegetables; cover and let stand 10 minutes for the beef to heat through.

TIP

Browning half the meat before cooking saves time and does not sacrifice flavor.

SERVES 6: About 300 calories, 34g protein, 15g carbohydrates, 11g fat (5g saturated), 2g fiber, 390mg sodium.

Stout-Braised Pot Roast with Carrots & Parsnips

The assertive flavor of the beer provides depth and flavor to this tasty gravy and acts as a nice counterbalance to the sweetness of the vegetables.

PREP: 25 MINUTES   TOTAL: 2 HOURS

1 boneless beef chuck roast (3 to 3½ pounds), well trimmed

Kosher salt

½ teaspoon ground black pepper

Cooking spray

3 slices bacon, cut into ¾-inch pieces

1 large onion, chopped

1 stalk celery, chopped

1 bottle (12 ounces) stout beer

1 teaspoon chopped fresh rosemary

1 pound carrots, peeled and cut into 2-inch chunks

1 pound parsnips, peeled and cut into 2-inch chunks

3 tablespoons flour dissolved in ⅓ cup water

2 large sweet potatoes, peeled and cut into 1-inch chunks

1. Pat the beef dry with paper towels; season with 1 teaspoon salt and the pepper. In the Instant Pot, select the sauté function and adjust the heat to more. Heat the pot for 1 to 2 minutes. Coat the bottom of the pot with cooking spray.

2. Add the bacon to the pot and cook, uncovered, for 4 minutes, or until browned. Using a slotted spoon, transfer it to paper towels to drain. Add the beef to the pot and cook 10 minutes, or until browned, turning once. Hit cancel to turn off the sauté function. Remove the beef to a plate. Add the onion and celery to the pot, scraping up any browned bits from the bottom. Add the beer, rosemary, and 1 teaspoon salt. Return the beef and any juices to the pot, pressing down to submerge it.

3. Cover and lock the lid. Select Manual/Pressure Cook and cook at high pressure for 1 hour 10 minutes. Once cooking is complete, release the pressure by using the natural release function for 10 minutes, then release the remaining pressure using a quick release. Place the roast on a cutting board and cover with foil.

4. Add the carrots and parsnips to the pot. Cover and lock the lid. Select Manual/Pressure Cook and cook at high pressure for 4 minutes. Release the pressure using a quick release. Using a slotted spoon, place the vegetables on a platter. Skim off any excess fat from the liquid in the pot. Choose the sauté function and adjust the heat to more.

5. Gradually add the dissolved flour mixture until blended and thickening. Add the sweet potatoes and simmer for 10 minutes, or until the potatoes are fork-tender. Meanwhile, slice the beef across the grain and place on the platter with the vegetables. Using a slotted spoon, place the potatoes around the beef. Finely chop the bacon and stir it into gravy. Serve with beef and vegetables.

SERVES 10: About 295 calories, 33g protein, 21g carbohydrates, 8g fat (3g saturated), 4g fiber, 521mg sodium.

Hungarian Pork Goulash

Even if you are not a sauerkraut fan, give this a try, as the fermented cabbage mellows while it cooks and combines with the other ingredients. Serve the finished dish over boiled potatoes or noodles, and top with additional sour cream, if desired.

PREP: 15 MINUTES   TOTAL: 1 HOUR 10 MINUTES

1 tablespoon bacon fat or vegetable oil

2 large onions (12 ounces each), coarsely chopped (4 cups)

Kosher salt

3 tablespoons paprika, preferably sweet Hungarian

3 cloves garlic, crushed with a garlic press

2 pounds lean boneless pork shoulder (Boston butt), trimmed and cut into 1½-inch pieces (1¾ pounds trimmed weight)

1 package (16 ounces) sauerkraut, drained and pressed to remove excess moisture

1 large tomato, coarsely chopped (1 cup)

½ cup lower-sodium beef broth

2 tablespoons packed brown sugar

½ teaspoon ground black pepper

½ cup light sour cream

1 tablespoon all-purpose flour

1. In the Instant Pot, select the sauté function. Add the bacon fat, onions, and ½ teaspoon salt; cook 10 minutes, or until golden, stirring frequently. Hit cancel to turn off the sauté function. Stir in the paprika and garlic, scraping up any browned bits from the bottom of the pot.

2. Stir in the pork, sauerkraut, tomato, broth, brown sugar, pepper, and ¾ teaspoon salt. Cover and lock the lid. Select Manual/Pressure Cook and cook at high pressure for 30 minutes. Release the pressure by using the natural release function for 15 minutes, then release the remaining pressure using a quick release.

3. In a small bowl, whisk the sour cream and flour together until blended. Select the sauté function and bring the mixture to a simmer. Stir in the sour cream mixture and simmer the goulash until thickened, about 1 minute.

SERVES 6: About 295 calories, 30g protein, 22g carbohydrates, 10g fat (4g saturated), 5g fiber, 858mg sodium.

White Bean Cassoulet with Pork & Lentils

Making traditional cassoulet is a long, laborious process. We've simplified it by cooking all the components in one pot at the same time, and the results are delicious! Lentils are not traditional, but they reduce the calories and up the fiber in this hearty meal.

PREP: 20 MINUTES   TOTAL: 1 HOUR, PLUS 10 MINUTES STANDING

2 slices thick-cut bacon, cut into 1-inch pieces

1 medium onion, chopped

3 tablespoons tomato paste

½ cup dry white wine

1⅓ pounds lean pork shoulder (Boston butt), trimmed of excess fat and cut into 2-inch pieces (about 1 pounds trimmed weight)

1½ cups lower-sodium chicken broth, homemade (page 37) or store-bought

1 can (14½ ounces) petite diced tomatoes, drained

8 cloves garlic, peeled and smashed

4 sprigs fresh thyme

½ cups brown lentils, rinsed and picked over

1 can (15 ounces) small white or great northern beans, rinsed and drained

½ teaspoon kosher salt

¼ teaspoon ground black pepper

Crusty bread, for serving (optional)

1. In the Instant Pot, using the sauté function, cook the bacon for 6 minutes, or until browned and crisp, stirring occasionally. Using a slotted spoon, transfer the bacon to a paper-towel-lined plate.

2. Add the onion to the pot and cook 3 minutes, or until softened, stirring occasionally. Stir in the tomato paste. Add the wine, stirring to scrape up any browned bits from the bottom of the pot. Hit cancel to turn off the sauté function.

3. Add the pork, broth, tomatoes, garlic, and thyme to the pot; stir to combine. Cover and lock the lid. Select Manual/Pressure Cook and cook at high pressure 25 minutes. Release the pressure by using a quick release. Stir in the lentils. Cover and lock the lid. Select Manual/Pressure Cook and cook at high pressure for 12 minutes. Once cooking is complete, release the pressure by using a quick release.

4. Discard the thyme sprigs. Gently stir in the beans, salt, pepper, and reserved bacon. Cover with the lid and let stand 10 minutes so the flavors combine and the beans heat through. Serve with crusty bread, if desired.

SERVES 4: About 375 calories, 37g protein, 42g carbohydrates, 6g fat (2g saturated), 14g fiber, 773mg sodium.

Pork & Peppers Ragù

It may seem unconventional, but browning only half of the pork saves time without sacrificing any flavor. Toss the ragù with cooked pasta or serve over polenta.

PREP: 30 MINUTES   TOTAL: 1 HOUR 35 MINUTES

1 large red bell pepper, sliced

1 large green bell pepper, sliced

2 tablespoons olive oil

3½ pounds boneless pork shoulder (Boston butt), trimmed of excess fat and cut into 2-inch chunks (2¾ pounds trimmed weight)

Kosher salt

1 large onion, coarsely chopped

3 tablespoons tomato paste

4 cloves garlic, chopped

½ cup dry red wine

1 cup canned crushed tomatoes

3 bay leaves

Ground black pepper

1 tablespoon balsamic vinegar

1. In the Instant Pot, using the sauté function, cook the bell peppers in 1 tablespoon of the oil for 5 minutes, or until slightly softened, stirring occasionally. Transfer the bell peppers to a bowl.

2. Pat the pork dry and season it on all sides with ½ teaspoon salt. Add the remaining 1 tablespoon oil and about one-fourth of the pork to the pot. Cook 5 minutes, or until browned on 2 sides, turning once. Transfer the pork to a plate. Repeat with another fourth of the pork, also transferring it to the plate when browned. To the pot, add the onion; cook 2 minutes, stirring occasionally. Add the tomato paste and garlic, stirring constantly. Add the wine and stir to scrape up any browned bits from the bottom of the pot. Hit cancel to turn off the sauté function.

3. Return the browned pork to the pot. Add the raw pork, crushed tomatoes, bay leaves, and ½ teaspoon pepper; stir well to combine. Cover and lock the lid. Select Manual/Pressure Cook and cook at high pressure for 30 minutes. Release the pressure using the natural release function for 15 minutes, then release the remaining pressure using a quick release.

4. With a slotted spoon, transfer the pork to a plate. Skim off any excess fat from the liquid in the pot and discard the bay leaves. Select the sauté function and bring the sauce to a boil. Stir in the bell peppers, 1 teaspoon salt, and ½ teaspoon pepper. Simmer 3 minutes, or until the bell peppers are tender. Hit cancel to turn off the sauté function.

5. With two forks, pull the pork into bite-size pieces. Return the pork and any juices to the pot; gently stir in the vinegar and let stand 5 minutes to heat through.

SERVES 10: About 225 calories, 20g protein, 7g carbohydrates, 12g fat (4g saturated), 2g fiber, 382mg sodium.

TIP

Serve the ragù with Creamy Cornmeal Polenta (page 63), a couple of sautéed vegetables (such as mushrooms and broccoli), grated Parmesan cheese, pesto, or other condiments that you desire.

CREAMY CORNMEAL POLENTA (page 63)

PORK & PEPPERS RAGÙ

Tomatillo Pork

This easy and flavorful dish can be sliced and sauced up to four days in advance, then microwaved à la minute.

PREP: 10 MINUTES   TOTAL: 1 HOUR 20 MINUTES

1 large bunch fresh cilantro

1 tablespoon vegetable oil

1 bone-in pork-shoulder roast (Boston butt; about 3 pounds), well trimmed

1 jar (16 to 18 ounces) mild salsa verde (green salsa)

3 cloves garlic, halved lengthwise

2 pounds small red potatoes (about 8), cut into quarters

1. From the cilantro, finely chop 1½ tablespoons of cilantro stems. Remove enough leaves from the remaining bunch to equal ½ cup, loosely packed, keeping it separate from the stems.

2. In the Instant Pot, select the sauté function and adjust the heat to more. Heat the oil for 1 to 2 minutes. Add the pork and cook it, uncovered, for 10 minutes, or until browned on both sides. Hit cancel to turn off the sauté function. Add 1 cup of the salsa, the garlic, and the chopped cilantro stems to the pot. Cover and lock the lid. Select Manual/Pressure Cook and cook at high pressure for 45 minutes. Once cooking is complete, release the pressure by using the natural release function for 20 minutes, then release the remaining pressure by using a quick release.

3. Transfer the pork to a cutting board. Add the potatoes to the pot. Cover and lock the lid. Select Manual/Pressure Cook and cook at high pressure for 5 minutes. Once cooking is complete, release the pressure by using a quick release. Meanwhile, slice the pork against the grain and place it on a platter; cover to keep warm. Using a slotted spoon, transfer the potatoes to the platter. Skim off the fat from the liquid in the pot and discard.

4. Select the sauté function and adjust the heat to more. Simmer for 10 minutes, or until the liquid is reduced by about one-third. Stir in the remaining salsa. Spoon the sauce over the pork and potatoes, and scatter the cilantro leaves on top.

SERVES 8: About 355 calories, 28g protein, 22g carbohydrates, 16g fat (5g saturated), 2g fiber, 539mg sodium.

Five-Spice Braised Pork & Bok Choy

Cubed tough cuts of pork become fork-tender in only 20 minutes!
Serve this flavorful meal over cooked rice noodles or
carrot noodles for a low-calorie change of pace.

PREP: 15 MINUTES   TOTAL: 50 MINUTES

1 orange

3½ pounds boneless pork shoulder, trimmed
and cut into 1½-inch pieces

1 large onion, chopped

1 (3-inch) piece peeled fresh ginger, cut into
slivers

1 cup lower-sodium chicken broth, homemade
(page 37) or store-bought

¼ cup lower-sodium soy sauce

2 tablespoons seasoned rice vinegar or cider
vinegar

2 tablespoons brown sugar

1 tablespoon Chinese five-spice powder

¾ teaspoon kosher salt

1¼ pounds baby bok choy, stems and leaves
separated and coarsely chopped

3 tablespoons cornstarch dissolved in
3 tablespoons water

Long-grain white rice, for serving (optional)

1. Peel three 3 × 1–inch strips of rind from the orange. Slice each crosswise into slivers. In the Instant Pot, combine the pork, onion, ginger, broth, soy sauce, vinegar, brown sugar, five-spice powder, salt, and orange peel slivers.

2. Cover and lock the lid. Select Manual/Pressure Cook and cook at high pressure for 20 minutes. Once cooking is complete, release the pressure using the natural release function for 10 minutes, then release the remaining pressure by using a quick release.

3. Skim off and discard any fat. Select the sauté function and bring the mixture to a simmer. Stir in the bok choy stems and cook 4 minutes. Stir the cornstarch mixture and gradually add it to the simmering stew. Stir in the bok choy leaves. Simmer until slightly thickened, about 1 minute. Serve with rice, if desired.

SERVES 8: About 270 calories, 26g protein, 13g carbohydrates, 12g fat (5g saturated), 2g fiber, 727mg sodium.

TIP

For an extra kick of orange flavor, add 1 teaspoon grated rind with the bok choy leaves in step 3.

Cuban-Style Pulled Pork with Olives

This fuss-free dish is the perfect make-ahead crowd-pleaser. You can cook the peppers for this recipe by bringing them up to pressure (set your Instant Pot for 00 minutes), then cancel the cooking with a quick release.

PREP: 15 MINUTES   TOTAL: 2 HOURS 20 MINUTES

1¼ cups lower-sodium beef broth

2 green bell peppers, seeded and sliced

¼ cup tomato paste

1 large onion, chopped

3 cloves garlic, chopped

¾ teaspoon kosher salt

1 tablespoon ground cumin

1 tablespoon dried oregano

1 boneless pork shoulder (about 4 pounds), trimmed of fat and cut into 3-inch chunks

1 cup pimiento-stuffed olives, sliced

1 tablespoon distilled white vinegar

Cilantro leaves, for garnish

8 cups cooked yellow rice, for serving

1. Combine the broth and bell peppers in the Instant Pot. Cover and lock the lid. Select Manual/Pressure Cook and cook at high pressure for 00 minutes. Once cooking is complete, release the pressure using the quick release function. Using a slotted spoon, transfer the bell peppers to a bowl.

2. Add the tomato paste, onion, garlic, salt, 2½ teaspoons of the cumin, and 2½ teaspoons of the oregano to the pot; stir to combine. Add the pork and press down to submerge in the liquid. Cover and lock the lid. Select Manual/Pressure Cook and cook at high pressure for 50 minutes. Once cooking is complete, release

the pressure using the natural release function for 15 minutes, then release the remaining pressure using a quick release. Select the keep warm function.

3. Transfer the pork to a cutting board. Skim off and discard any fat from the pot. Using two forks, shred the pork, removing any fat or gristle. Stir the pork back into pot, along with the olives, vinegar, the remaining ½ teaspoon cumin and ½ teaspoon oregano, and the cooked bell peppers. Cover and let stand 5 minutes, or until heated through. Garnish with cilantro and serve with yellow rice.

SERVES 10: About 340 calories, 25g protein, 31g carbohydrates, 12g fat (4g saturated), 2g fiber, 1,181mg sodium.

TIP

It might seem odd to set your Instant Pot to 00 minutes, but don't fret. The vegetables in this recipe will cook during the time the pot takes to build pressure. If you set your Instant Pot for more time, the vegetables will be overdone.

Pulled Pork Barbecue

You don't have to go crazy trimming the fat from the shoulder: As the meat cooks, the fat will melt, keeping the meat moist and tender. But before preparing the sauce, make sure to skim the fat from the cooking liquid. Serve the pulled pork on slider rolls.

PREP: 15 MINUTES   TOTAL: 1 HOUR 30 MINUTES

2 tablespoons smoked paprika

2 tablespoons packed dark brown sugar

1 teaspoon garlic powder

1 teaspoon onion powder

¾ teaspoon ground black pepper

Kosher salt

3½ pounds boneless pork shoulder (Boston butt), trimmed and cut into 4 pieces (3 pounds trimmed weight)

½ cup cider vinegar

¼ cup Worcestershire sauce

¼ cup water

1 cup ketchup

2 tablespoons spicy brown mustard

½ teaspoon crushed red pepper

1. In a cup, mix together the paprika, brown sugar, garlic powder, onion powder, pepper, and 1 teaspoon salt. Sprinkle the mixture over the pork and rub to coat.

2. In the Instant Pot, combine the cider vinegar, Worcestershire sauce, and water. Add the pork. Cover and lock the lid. Select Manual/Pressure Cook and cook at high pressure for 1 hour. Once cooking is complete, release the pressure by using the natural release function.

3. Using a slotted spoon, transfer the pork to a plate. Pour the cooking liquid into a bowl; skim off and discard the fat. Return 1 cup of the cooking liquid to the pot. Stir in the ketchup, mustard, and crushed red pepper. Select the sauté function and bring the sauce to a boil. Cook 4 minutes, or until the sauce thickens slightly and reduces to about 2 cups, stirring frequently. Hit cancel to turn off the sauté function. Reserve ¾ cup of the sauce and set it aside.

4. Using two forks, shred the pork, discarding any pieces of visible fat. Stir the pork and ½ teaspoon salt into the pot. Let stand 5 minutes. Serve with the reserved sauce.

SERVES 16 SLIDERS: About 250 calories, 17g protein, 28g carbohydrates, 9g fat (2g saturated), 1g fiber, 566mg sodium.

> **TIP**
>
> Reserve the extra cooking liquid to moisten the pulled pork if needed.

Baby Back Ribs

These ribs cook to tender perfection in only 20 minutes!
If you can't find baby back ribs, you can use a 3-pound rack of
St. Louis ribs, but adjust the cooking time to 30 minutes.

PREP: 15 MINUTES   TOTAL: 55 MINUTES

2 racks baby back ribs (1½ pounds each), each rack cut in half

2 tablespoons packed brown sugar

1 tablespoon smoked paprika

1 teaspoon chipotle chili powder

1 teaspoon kosher salt

½ teaspoon garlic powder

¼ teaspoon ground black pepper

¾ cup water

½ cup barbecue sauce, plus more (optional), for serving

1. Using paper towels, pat the ribs dry. Remove the white membrane from the bone side of the ribs. In a bowl, mix together the brown sugar, paprika, chili powder, salt, garlic powder, and pepper. Rub the spice mixture on both sides of the ribs.

2. In the Instant Pot, insert the steamer rack and add the water. Stand the ribs on their sides in the pot, with 3 around the side of the pot and 1 in the center. Cover and lock the lid. Select Manual/Pressure Cook and cook on high pressure for 20 minutes. Release the pressure using the natural release function for 10 minutes, then release the remaining pressure by using a quick release. Remove the ribs to a foil-lined sheet pan.

3. Adjust an oven rack 3 to 4 inches from the broiler and preheat it. Brush the ribs with ¼ cup of the barbecue sauce and broil for about 3 minutes, or until glazed. Turn and repeat with the remaining ¼ cup sauce. Serve with additional sauce, if desired.

SERVES 6: About 370 calories, 25g protein, 15g carbohydrates, 23g fat (8g saturated), 1g fiber, 668mg sodium.

SAUCY SHRIMP CREOLE
(PAGE 115)

6 | Fish

It's true—fish and shellfish cook pretty quickly, whatever your cooking method. What the Instant Pot does so well is lock in flavor, so you get rich broth for your Cioppino and plump juicy mussels, whether you cook them Spanish-style or with tomatoes and white wine. Salmon steams beautifully in the pot. Serve it cold with a watercress sauce or a hot-and-spicy hoisin glaze—you'll get moist, evenly cooked fish every time. The Instant Pot is also an excellent rice cooker, so you'll turn out a delicious shrimp-and-sausage Jambalaya. The Instant Pot is an easy way to capture the flavors of the catch of the day.

Cioppino

This Italian-American fish stew originates in San Francisco. If you like a little heat, add a pinch of crushed red pepper to the onion mixture while sautéing.

PREP: 20 MINUTES   TOTAL: 1 HOUR 5 MINUTES

1 bottle (8 ounces) clam juice

2 pounds mussels, scrubbed

2 tablespoons olive oil

1 fennel bulb, chopped

1 medium onion, finely chopped

3 cloves garlic, crushed with a garlic press

½ teaspoon kosher salt

¼ teaspoon ground black pepper

1 can (28 ounces) crushed tomatoes

2 tablespoons butter

1 pound boneless cod fillet, cut into 2-inch chunks

1 pound shelled, deveined shrimp with tails left on (21 to 25 count)

Chopped parsley or basil, for garnish

Crusty bread, for serving

1. In the Instant Pot, combine the clam juice and mussels. Cover and lock the lid. Select Manual/Pressure Cook and cook at high pressure for 2 minutes. Release the pressure by using a quick release function. Using a slotted spoon, transfer the mussels to a bowl. Discard any mussels that do not open. Cover the mussels to keep warm. Pour the mussel broth from the pot into a small bowl and set aside. Rinse and dry the pot.

2. Select the sauté function and heat the oil for 1 to 2 minutes. Add the fennel and onion and cook for 3 minutes, or until softened, stirring occasionally. Stir in the garlic, salt, and pepper.

Hit cancel to turn off the sauté function. Stir in the crushed tomatoes, butter, and reserved mussel broth, leaving any sediment in the bottom of the bowl. Cover and lock the lid. Select Manual/Pressure Cook and cook at high pressure for 7 minutes. Once cooking is complete, release the pressure by using a quick release.

3. Select the sauté function and adjust the heat to less. Stir in the cod, partially cover with the lid, and cook for 2 minutes. Gently stir in the shrimp, partially cover with the lid, and cook for 2 to 3 minutes, or until the shrimp are just opaque, gently stirring once. Hit cancel to turn off the sauté function. Return the mussels to the pot without stirring. Partially cover with the lid and let stand 5 minutes to heat the mussels through. Sprinkle each serving with parsley and serve with crusty bread.

SERVES 6: About 320 calories, 36g protein, 18g carbohydrates, 12g fat (4g saturated), 4g fiber, 1,200mg sodium.

TIP

If you buy shrimp in the shell, you will need 1¼ pounds to equal 1 pound once they are shelled and deveined.

Saucy Shrimp Creole

Many seasoning blends are loaded with salt, so if you can't find a salt-free blend, make your own: Combine five parts paprika with one part each dried basil, cayenne pepper, garlic powder, onion powder, dried oregano, ground black pepper, and dried thyme.

PREP: 20 MINUTES   TOTAL: 50 MINUTES

3 tablespoons butter, softened

2 stalks celery, finely chopped

1 large green bell pepper, finely chopped

1 medium onion, finely chopped

1½ teaspoons salt-free Creole seasoning

1 bottle (8 ounces) clam juice

2 medium tomatoes, coarsely chopped

2 tablespoons all-purpose flour

1½ pounds peeled, deveined large (25 to 30 count) shrimp

1 tablespoon Worcestershire sauce

1 tablespoon Louisiana-style hot sauce, or more to taste

¾ teaspoon kosher salt, or more to taste

1½ cups white rice, cooked, for serving

1. In the Instant Pot, using sauté function, heat 1 tablespoon of the butter for 1 to 2 minutes, or until melted. Add the celery, bell pepper, and onion; cook 3 minutes, or until softened, stirring occasionally. Stir in the Creole seasoning. Add the clam juice and top it all with the tomatoes; do not stir. Hit cancel to turn off the sauté function.

2. Cover and lock the lid. Select Manual/Pressure Cook and cook at high pressure for 5 minutes. Meanwhile, mix the remaining 2 tablespoons butter and the flour on a plate using a fork to make a smooth paste.

3. Once cooking is complete, release the pressure by using a quick release. Select the sauté function and bring the vegetables to a simmer. Stir in the flour mixture; simmer the sauce 1 minute, or until thickened, stirring. Stir in the shrimp, Worcestershire sauce, hot sauce, and salt. Replace the lid to slightly ajar and simmer 3 minutes, or until the shrimp are just opaque, stirring occasionally. With pot holders, remove the hot insert from the pot to stop the cooking. Cover and let stand 1 minute. Taste and add additional hot sauce and/or salt if needed. Serve over rice.

SERVES 6: About 355 calories, 21g protein, 51g carbohydrates, 9g fat (5g saturated), 2g fiber, 915mg sodium.

Jambalaya

Jambalaya uses the holy trinity of Cajun cooking: onion, green bell pepper, and celery. Smoked kielbasa makes a good substitute if you have trouble finding andouille sausage.

PREP: 20 MINUTES   TOTAL: 50 MINUTES, PLUS STANDING

8 ounces fully cooked andouille sausage, sliced

2 teaspoons canola oil

1 pound medium (31 to 40 count) shrimp, shelled and deveined

1 medium onion, chopped

1 green bell pepper, chopped

1 large stalk celery, chopped

3 cloves garlic, finely chopped

¾ teaspoon kosher salt

¼ teaspoon dried thyme

⅛ to ¼ teaspoon cayenne pepper

¼ cup water

1½ cups long-grain white rice, rinsed and drained

1 can (14½ ounces) chicken broth or 1¾ cups homemade (page 37)

1 can (14½ ounces) diced tomatoes

2 green onions, thinly sliced

Hot sauce, for serving (optional)

1. In the Instant Pot, select the sauté function and heat for 1 to 2 minutes. Spray the pot with cooking spray, add the sausage, and cook 4 minutes, stirring occasionally, until lightly browned. Transfer to a bowl.

2. Add the oil to the pot and cook the shrimp 1 minute, or until just beginning to turn pink but not cooked through, stirring. Transfer the shrimp to a plate.

3. Add the onion, bell pepper, and celery to the pot. Cook 4 minutes, or until softening, stirring frequently. Stir in the garlic, salt, thyme, and cayenne. Hit cancel to turn off the sauté function. Add the water and stir well to scrape up any browned bits from the bottom of the pot. Stir in the rice, broth, tomatoes, and sausage. Cover and lock the lid. Select Manual/Pressure Cook and cook at high pressure for 7 minutes. Once cooking is complete, release the pressure by using a quick release.

4. Stir in the shrimp, cover the pot with the lid slightly ajar, and let stand 10 minutes to finish cooking the shrimp. Sprinkle with green onions and serve with hot sauce, if desired.

SERVES 6: About 345 calories, 19g protein, 48g carbohydrates, 8g fat (2g saturated), 2g fiber, 1,113mg sodium.

Cold Poached Salmon with Watercress Sauce

The Instant Pot perfectly cooks this heart-healthy fish in 4 minutes. To prevent sticking, we line the steamer rack with onion slices, which also add flavor.

PREP: 15 MINUTES   TOTAL: 25 MINUTES, PLUS COOLING

1 medium lemon

1 cup water

1 medium onion, thinly sliced

4 salmon fillets, 1 inch thick (6 ounces each)

¾ teaspoon kosher salt

½ teaspoon ground black pepper

Watercress Sauce (right)

1. From the lemon, squeeze the juice, reserving it for the Watercress Sauce. Cut the lemon shell into fourths and place them in the Instant Pot. Set the steamer rack in the pot and add the water. Arrange the onion slices on the steamer rack. Place the salmon, skin side down, on the onions and season with the salt and pepper.

2. Cover and lock the lid. Select Manual/Pressure Cook and cook at high pressure for 3 minutes. Once cooking is complete, release the pressure by using a quick release. Check the salmon at the thickest part for doneness (if necessary, return it to the pot, cover, and let stand 2 to 3 minutes longer). Remove the rack from the pot and, using a spatula, transfer the salmon to a platter. Let cool 30 minutes, or cover and refrigerate to serve later.

3. Meanwhile, prepare the Watercress Sauce. To serve, remove the skin from the salmon and serve with the sauce.

SERVES 4 (with 2 tablespoons sauce): About 275 calories, 30g protein, 0g carbohydrates, 16g fat (3g saturated), 0g fiber, 231mg sodium.

Watercress Sauce

In a blender or in a food processor with the knife blade attached, puree **½ bunch watercress**, tough stems trimmed (1 cup); **½ cup sour cream**; **1 tablespoon fresh lemon juice**; **1 teaspoon chopped fresh tarragon or ⅛ teaspoon dried tarragon**; **1½ teaspoons sugar**; and **1 teaspoon kosher salt** until smooth. Cover and refrigerate if not using immediately. Makes about ½ cup.

SERVES 4: About 55 calories, 1g protein, 3g carbohydrates, 5g fat (2g saturated), 0g fiber, 491mg sodium.

Spanish Moules Frites

Pressure-steaming mussels and clams provides
perfectly even cooking throughout.

PREP: 20 MINUTES   TOTAL: 45 MINUTES

1 package (26 ounces) frozen French fries

½ teaspoon smoked paprika

½ tablespoon olive or vegetable oil

1 medium onion, chopped

3 ounces dried chorizo, quartered lengthwise
  and thinly sliced

2 cloves garlic, finely chopped

1 can (14½ ounces) diced tomatoes

¾ cup dry white wine

4 pounds large mussels, scrubbed and
  debearded (see Tip)

2 tablespoons chopped fresh parsley

1. Prepare the fries as the label directs. Toss with the paprika once they are cooked, and keep warm.

2. Meanwhile, in the Instant Pot, select the sauté function and heat the oil for 1 to 2 minutes. Add the onion and cook, uncovered, for 5 minutes, or until softened. Add the chorizo and garlic. Cook 1 minute, stirring occasionally. Stir in the tomatoes with their juices and the wine.

3. Add the mussels to the pot. Cover and lock the lid. Select Manual/Pressure Cook and cook at high pressure for 3 minutes. Once cooking is complete, release the pressure by using a quick release. Transfer the mussels to a large shallow bowl. Discard any mussels that do not open. Pour the mussel broth over the mussels and sprinkle with parsley. Serve with the fries.

SERVES 8: About 280 calories, 19g protein, 27g carbohydrates, 10g fat (3g saturated), 3g fiber, 657mg sodium.

Mussels with Tomatoes & White Wine

Omit the French fries and smoked paprika. Prepare the mussels as directed, also omitting the chorizo and adding ¼ **teaspoon crushed red pepper** with the tomatoes and wine in step 2.

SERVES 8: About 130 calories, 14g protein, 9g carbohydrates, 3g fat (1g saturated), 1g fiber, 441mg sodium.

> **TIP**
>
> To clean mussels, scrub them well under cold running water. Then grasp the hairlike beard firmly with your thumb and forefinger and pull it away, or scrape it off with a knife. Cultivated mussels usually do not have beards.

Hoisin-Glazed Salmon

Perfect for multitasking, you can quick-cook your vegetables in the bottom of the Instant Pot while your salmon is prepared on the steamer rack. For a milder flavor, substitute half a thin-sliced red bell pepper for some of the jalapeños.

PREP: 15 MINUTES   TOTAL: 30 MINUTES

5 stalks celery, thinly sliced

4 red jalapeño chilies, seeded and thinly sliced

1 bunch green onions, sliced, white and green parts separated, plus more for garnish

⅓ cup water

4 skinless salmon fillets (6 ounces each)

1 tablespoon hoisin sauce

2 teaspoons honey

2 teaspoons rice wine vinegar

Bok choy, steamed, for serving

¼ cup unsalted peanuts, chopped, for garnish

1. Combine the celery, jalapeños, white ends of the green onions, and water in the Instant Pot. Spread them in an even layer and place the steamer rack on top. Coat the rack with cooking spray.

2. Arrange the salmon on the rack, alternating the thick and thin ends to fit. Combine the hoisin and honey in a small dish. Spoon and spread 3 teaspoons over the salmon. Stir the rice vinegar into the remaining mixture and set it aside.

3. Cover and lock the lid. Select Manual/Pressure Cook and cook at high pressure for 3 minutes. Once cooking is complete, release the pressure by using a quick release. Check the salmon at the thickest part for doneness (return to the pot, cover, and let stand 2 to 3 minutes more if needed). Remove the rack with the salmon. Toss the reserved green onions with the celery mixture. Remove the mixture with a slotted spoon and serve it with the salmon, bok choy, and reserved sauce. Garnish with peanuts and green onions.

SERVES 4: About 360 calories, 42g protein, 12g carbohydrates, 16g fat (3g saturated), 3g fiber, 187mg sodium.

Index

Note: Page numbers in *italics* indicate photos separate from recipes.

Photography Credits

Metric Conversion Charts

The recipes that appear in this cookbook use the standard United States method for measuring liquid and dry or solid ingredients (teaspoons, tablespoons, and cups). The information on this chart is provided to help cooks outside the U.S. successfully use these recipes. All equivalents are approximate.

METRIC EQUIVALENTS FOR DIFFERENT TYPES OF INGREDIENTS

STANDARD CUP	FINE POWDER (e.g., flour)	GRAIN (e.g., rice)	GRANULAR (e.g., sugar)	LIQUID SOLIDS (e.g., butter)	LIQUID (e.g., milk)
¾	105 g	113 g	143 g	150 g	180 ml
⅔	93 g	100 g	125 g	133 g	160 ml
½	70 g	75 g	95 g	100 g	120 ml
⅓	47 g	50 g	63 g	67 g	80 ml
¼	35 g	38 g	48 g	50 g	60 ml
⅛	18 g	19 g	24 g	25 g	30 ml

¼ tsp	=						1 ml
½ tsp	=						2 ml
1 tsp	=						5 ml
3 tsp	=	1 tbsp	=		½ fl oz	=	15 ml
		2 tbsp	=	⅛ cup	=	1 fl oz	=	30 ml
		4 tbsp	=	¼ cup	=	2 fl oz	=	60 ml
		5⅓ tbsp	=	⅓ cup	=	3 fl oz	=	80 ml
		8 tbsp	=	½ cup	=	4 fl oz	=	120 ml
		10⅔ tbsp	=	⅔ cup	=	5 fl oz	=	160 ml
		12 tbsp	=	¾ cup	=	6 fl oz	=	180 ml
		16 tbsp	=	1 cup	=	8 fl oz	=	240 ml
		1 pt	=	2 cups	=	16 fl oz	=	480 ml
		1 qt	=	4 cups	=	32 fl oz	=	960 ml
						33 fl oz	=	1000 ml = 1 L

USEFUL EQUIVALENTS FOR DRY INGREDIENTS BY WEIGHT

(To convert ounces to grams, multiply the number of ounces by 30.)

1 oz	=	¹⁄₁₆ lb	=	30 g
2 oz	=	¼ lb	=	120 g
4 oz	=	½ lb	=	240 g
8 oz	=	¾ lb	=	360 g
16 oz	=	1 lb	=	480 g

USEFUL EQUIVALENTS LENGTH

(To convert inches to centimeters, multiply the number of inches by 2.5.)

1 in	=		2.5 cm	
6 in	= ½ ft =		15 cm	
12 in	= 1 ft =		30 cm	
36 in	= 3 ft = 1 yd =		90 cm	
40 in	=		100 cm	= 1 m

USEFUL EQUIVALENTS FOR COOKING/OVEN TEMPERATURES

	Fahrenheit	Celsius	Gas Mark
Freeze Water	32°F	0°C	
Room Temperature	68°F	20°C	
Boil Water	212°F	100°C	
Bake	325°F	160°C	3
	350°F	180°C	4
	375°F	190°C	5
	400°F	200°C	6
	425°F	220°C	7
	450°F	230°C	8
Broil			Grill

TESTED 'TIL PERFECT

Each and every recipe is developed in the Good Housekeeping Test Kitchen, where our team of culinary geniuses create, test, and continue to test recipes until they're perfect. (Even if we make the same dish ten times!)